Republished in 2018
First Published in 2017
002
Requests for permission to reproduce material from this work should be sent to the Author directly at:

15 Stratton Street
London
W1J 8LQ

Jacket Art: Author's own work. "English Landscape in May", Dhruv Sharma.

Copyright © Dhruv Sharma, 2017, 2018

The moral right of the author has been asserted. In addition Dhruv Sharma has asserted his right under the Copyright, Designs and Patents Act, 1988, to be identified as Author of this work.

A CIP Catalogue record for this book is available from the British Library.

Type Set in 6, 7, 8, 9, 12, 14, 24 pt Georgia

ISBN: 978-1973410126
ISBN: 978-1728649672

10 9 8 7 6 5 4 3 2 1

Observations on U.S., Japanese, and German Forex Interventions, 1973-2004

Contents

Preface	8
Chapter 1	14
Chapter 2	28
Chapter 3	66
Chapter 4	83
Chapter 5	96
Chapter 6	113
Chapter 7	125
Chapter 8	153
References	159

Preface

"the foreign exchange market is a herd of steers, and central banks are herd dogs"

Dominguez and Frankel

Following the collapse of Bretton Woods initiated by the 'Nixon Shock' in 1971, a new International Monetary System was born in which a nexus of floating currencies were controlled with the supposed intention to provide stability for the Global Economy by adapting the activist policy intervention of earlier Monetary Standards; such as the Bretton Woods, Interwar Years, and Classical Gold Standards.

The three dominant economies of the new monetary order following Bretton Woods Collapse were the U.S., Japan, and Germany; together these G-3 Economies influenced exchange-rate determination and volatility during Post Bretton Woods by directly spending a combined total of $963 billion, from 1973 to 2004, to 'dirty' manage their currencies so as to determine world trade and thereby global economic output.

In this book, I provide novel observations into the impact of Foreign Exchange Interventions on exchange-rate volatility and determination of the G-3 Economies during Post Bretton Woods. I use SVAR modelling to demonstrate the evolution of Interventionist Policy Regimes. More importantly, I define these Policy Regimes from Primary Sources and Documents. I combine previously overlapping and disparate elements of Macroeconomic History and International Economics; justifying estimation techniques with an underlying broad and methodological narrative which is otherwise absent from previous works. Much of the work, analysis, and research for this book was carried out in 2012 by the Author.

Successful Interventionist Regimes only came to prolong Post Bretton Woods Interventions and the pursuit of exchange rate stability was ultimately a mirage; primary sources reveal that for it remain an objective of G-3 policymakers in Post Bretton Woods for so long is all the more surprising given policymakers' early consensual scepticism towards the effectiveness of government intervention on exchange rates. Using combined narrative and econometric approaches, I demonstrate the evolution of Interventions and their corresponding effects on exchange rates; the combination of the two approaches portrays well the final death knell to pervasive Currency Interventions, at least amongst most Western policymakers till the onset of the 2008 U.S. Financial Crisis.

Foreign Exchange, hereafter Forex, Interventions conducted by U.S., Japan, and Germany (West Germany before 1990) during Post Bretton Woods were for all intents and purposes an unprecedented attempt to bring the policy influence of past Monetary Systems to the one created following the collapse of Bretton Woods; furthermore, Post Bretton Woods was a unique period in economic history for the experimental nature of its economic policy. I broadly define Post Bretton Woods from 1973 to 2007, from the collapse of the Smithsonian Agreement to the beginning of the 2007-08 U.S. Financial Crisis; for the purposes of this book, I focus on the following time periods for U.S., Japan, and Germany: 1973:3-1995:12, 1973:3-2004:10, and 1973:3-1995:12, respectively.

At its simplest policymakers conduct Forex Interventions in order to influence the value and behaviour of the exchange rate. Exchange rate Determination in Post Bretton Woods has been conducted mostly through financial markets however with considerable herding and guidance coming from Policymakers. Dominguez and Frankel, in *Does Foreign Exchange Intervention Work?*, have described this relationship as "the foreign exchange market is a herd of steers, and central banks are herd dogs. They bark and nip at the heels of the steers, with the aim of moving the herd in the desired direction".

However, in a stylised *Weltanschauung* of open-economy macroeconomics, Purchasing Power Parity and Uncovered Interest-rate Parity have been the traditional building blocks of a flexible exchange rate system. Uncovered Interest-rate Parity holds when profitable returns available on relative interest rates differential between two economies exist, they are negated by adjustments in the bilateral exchange rate; Purchasing Power Parity holds real exchange rate constant as differences in relative inflation rates leads to corresponding adjustments in the nominal bilateral exchange rate.

In this view, markets freely determine exchange rates through adjustments to differences in productivity, inflation, economic growth, and other macroeconomic variables. Furthermore, efforts to influence the exchange-rate through government action, to correct a perceived market failure or to address a political bloc or industrial constituency, would be unsuccessful given the limited amount of Forex Reserves compared to the much larger daily turnover of the Forex Market, the latter volumes increased exponentially over Post Bretton Woods. However, in this book, I reconcile theory with actual practice of pervasive Government Interventions. I proceed in several steps within this book; Chapter 1 lays out the groundwork for the narrative; Chapter 2 provides an overview on U.S. Forex Interventions; Chapter 3 on Japanese Forex Interventions; Chapter 4 on German Forex Interventions; Chapter 5 analyses policy motivations for Forex Interventions; Chapter 6 provides a literature review; Chapter 7 gives empirical results; and Chapter 8 summarizes.

October 2017
Dhruv Sharma

Chapter 1

"Remember, the other central banks have done the same thing, following our doing it. The Germans most recently, and the Japanese too, have been operating in a discreet manner"

Cross

There are two types of Forex Interventions. Firstly, Unsterilised Forex Intervention is akin to an open market operation. The Intervention becomes unsterilised if the change in the policymakers' net foreign currency assets is met by a corresponding change in their monetary liabilities. Unsterilised Interventions are similar to the theoretical monetary equilibrium created with Gold flows in the Classical Gold Standard during the 19th Century, leading up to to World War I.

Unsterilised Interventions introduces a new element of exchange rate targeting into the central bank's reaction function, which leads to a trade-off between domestic and exchange rate objectives. In the open-macroeconomic framework unsterilised Interventions are effective due to their positive influence on the market interest rates.

And then, secondly, there is Sterilised Forex Interventions, which does not change the level of the monetary base due to counter operations by policymakers in the bond markets, offsetting the change in net-foreign assets. Policymakers choose to sterilise the Intervention by selling government debt through open-market operations to the non-banking private sector. This mops extra liquidity and so leaves the money supply unchanged. However, if the sales of extra debt push market interest rates up, this offsets the effects of Intervention on the exchange rate making the Intervention self-defeating. Sterilised Interventions reinforce central bank monetary policy independence.

A Sterilised Intervention has two principal transmission mechanisms into the real economy. Firstly, through the portfolio balance mechanism a spot depreciation occurs to compensate risk-averse investors on the perceived risk of more abundant and imperfectly substitutable securities denominated in the sterilised and selling currency. In the Portfolio Mechanism, for instance, the Fed would liquidate its Yen-denominated bonds and concomitantly buy domestic Dollar-denominated bonds, leaving the monetary base and interest rates unaffected. Due to the relative increase in Yen/Dollar Debt, investors would demand a higher expected return on yen debt which may occur through a bilateral exchange rate adjustment.

The portfolio mechanism assumes there are unrestricted cross-border financial flows and the absence of Ricardian equivalence. Under Ricardian Equivalence private agents offset any effects of Intervention because domestic and foreign bonds are perfectly substitutable. Additionally, Sterilised Interventions are typically too small to significantly influence the relative quantities of bonds. The Inventory adjustment is a micro level variant of the portfolio mechanism; this mechanism uses order flows to transmit private information into the price during the trading process.

Secondly, the other transmission mechanism for Sterilised Intervention occurs through the expectations mechanism, acting through informational asymmetry and non-fundamental forces which affect the price of the exchange rate in the Forex markets by influencing private agents' assessment of the equilibrium level of the exchange rate.

Generally, Sterilised Forex Interventions provide a buffer to policymakers from compromising their domestic monetary policy objectives. However, there is another mechanism through which Sterilised Forex Interventions have an effect on exchange rates: Signalling.

Mussa in 'The Role of Official Intervention', *Group of Thirty*, argued a central bank may signal unanticipated changes in monetary policy through Forex Interventions leading to exchange rate changes as private agents adjust to new intervention-related information. The signal is credible because the central bank would incur a capital loss on its Forex position if it fails to carry through with the policy change. The Signalling mechanism does not offer the scope for central banks to independently maintain and pursue both dual exchange rate and domestic objectives, since interventions through sales of a foreign currency signals a compatible monetary contraction. In general, Bordo, Humpage, and Schwartz, argue Sterilised Interventions do not provide policymakers with the systematic tools independent of their monetary policy to influence exchange rates.

Secret, hereafter Closed, Interventions mitigates the involvement of speculation; however, Closed Interventions by definition negate the exercise of the expectations and signalling channels to influence the exchange rate. Nevertheless, Closed Interventions are appropriate when they are inconsistent with other macroeconomic policies and would otherwise undermine central bank credibility and interest rate policy; U.S. Policymakers at times felt Closed Interventions were more effective for instance as argued in the FOMC Meeting which occurred on the 5th-6th July 1989 between Wayne Angell, Governor of the Federal Reserve Board between 1986 and 1994, and Sam Cross, Manager for Foreign Operations for the Federal Reserve System Open Market Account between 1980s and 1991:

"MR. ANGELL. Sam, to what extent did you use banks to execute the orders in such a manner that the market would not have immediately recognized it as a central bank order?

MR. CROSS. Well, during this period we did most of it in what we call a discreet manner. That is to say, we operated through a bank acting as an agent so that--although the word does get around in some way and people who are following these markets closely can often tell a lot of what's going on--we did not go in openly buying foreign currencies. For the most part we had particular banks operating on our behalf in order not to show the extent to which the central banks were in there. We had gotten to a point where operating visibly was not really working very effectively and we thought it would be better to operate this way. Indeed, it has been much more successful. Remember, the other central banks have done the same thing, following our doing it. The Germans most recently, and the Japanese too, have been operating in a discreet manner.
MR. ANGELL. Do you think you were able to buy more cheaply by buying discreetly than if you had bought openly? Did you buy the portfolio--

MR. CROSS. I think it was a lot more effective because we had reached a point where the market tended to feel that these rates were out of control-- well, not out of control but beyond the ranges that the authorities wanted. And when they saw the central bank coming in there they almost took that as a basis [for believing] that the dollar was by definition undervalued. And they tended to hit it quickly. Now, in operating more discreetly we have been able to kind of encourage the dollar down without appearing to try to take on the market in a direct way. Under certain conditions one technique is more appropriate and under other circumstances another way is. We have felt during this period, given the market conditions that we faced, that this was the better way to operate. And I think that has proved to be the case."

The time inconsistency problem of Forex Interventions occurs when publically announced, hereafter Open, Forex Interventions may trigger speculative activity which may make the interventions ex post costly and counterproductive. This effect is more pronounced for shallow and illiquid Forex markets, in particular the currencies of developing economies in Post Bretton Woods. Sarno and Taylor conclude Open Interventions are effective provided they are consistent with the underlying stance of monetary and fiscal policy. However, the Jurgensen report from 1983 reported U.S. policymakers in the 1970s noted short-term effectiveness of Interventions was undermined by a lack of concomitant measures to deal with the underlying causes of the Dollar's movement.

Another mechanism through which policymakers influence behaviour is through public statements about the desired level of the exchange rate, which are not accompanied by subsequent Forex Interventions; often, 'oral Interventions' are made in response to small changes in the exchange rate, preceding an actual Intervention.. On one unique occasion, in January 1978, the Federal Reserve and the U.S. Treasury issued a joint statement for imminent Forex Intervention, followed by the New York Desk's 'phantom' offers of Deutschmarks, this prompted private speculators to purchase dollars leading to a self-fulfilling outcome; Federal Reserve Bulletin, March 1978:

"On January 4 the Federal Reserve and the U.S. Treasury issued a joint statement:

The Exchange Stabilization Fund of the United States Treasury will henceforth be utilized actively together with the $20 billion swap network operated by the Federal Reserve System . A swap agreement has just been reached by the Treasury with the Deutsche Bundesbank and is already in force. Joint intervention by the Treasury, the Federal Reserve, and foreign central banks is designed to check speculation and reestablish order in the foreign exchange markets.

When this statement came across the news services early that afternoon, the Federal Reserve's foreign exchange Trading Desk followed up with simultaneous offers of marks to several banks in the New York market. This prompted a quick scramble for cover by some professionals who were short of dollars, and the mark dropped back by some 4 per cent that afternoon without the Desk actually having sold any marks. Some further short covering during the next morning in Frankfurt pushed the mark even lower to $0.4640."

Finally, in this Chapter, it is important to observe some G-3 Forex Interventions in Post Bretton Woods hitherto have remained unpublished; most policymakers continue to keep the size and time of Interventions unpublished to avoid weakening their current and future credibility in case those interventions are shown to be ex post ineffective. *The Wall Street Journal*, 8th August 2000, observed:

"By showing that money spent for currency intervention has often had the opposite of its desired effect in the long-term, intervention data could make [policymakers] less prone to intervening so often"

Nevertheless, qualitative information on Closed and unpublished Interventions can be estimated through primary sources. Absolute Nominal Dollar Amount of published G-3 Forex Interventions sum $807 billion over Post Bretton Woods; and total Interventions, both my estimations and published, amount to $963 billion between 1973:03-2004:03 from my own calculations in the following pages. However in existing econometric studies of Forex Interventions, the selection bias is towards published Intervention data. Furthermore, some empirical studies on Forex Interventions use changes in reserves as a proxy for Interventions.

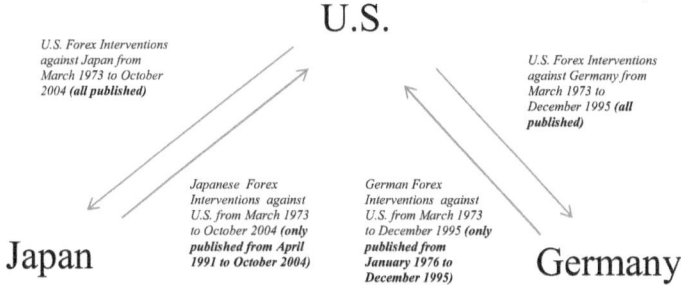

Figure 1: Schematic Outline of Published G-3 Forex Interventions in Post Bretton Woods.

In Figure 1, I outline the bilateral range of monthly time series of G-3 Forex Interventions used in this Book. With the time periods actually published in bold. I will estimate Monthly Forex Interventions, which are hitherto unpublished, for Japan, 1973:3-1991:3, and Germany, 1973:3-1975:12. For both estimations I use changes in monthly Dollar Reserves as the Bundesbank and Bank of Japan were aiming to accumulate solely external assets in Dollars for Intervention purposes in these time periods; *Monthly Report of the Deutsche Bundesbank*, November 1988, p.30., observed:

"Only [...] US Financial Markets [...] offer an adequate guarantee that foreign exchange reserves will be available at any time"

For at least the German Estimates, 1973 till 1975, primary sources suggest sizeable changes in German External Dollar Reserves are a good proxy for German Interventions against the U.S. Additionally, to an extent daily forex noise is mitigated by using monthly, rather than daily, changes in Japanese and German Dollar-denominated Forex Levels. I qualify monthly noise, as may exist, in table 1 further by only using changes qualified to certain monthly thresholds. Inference is placed on these changes caused by actual Forex Interventions which is expanded further in Chapter 2. Primary evidence does however suggest that the U.S. intervened in modest, but large chunks. Sam Cross observed in the *FOMC Transcript*, 19th-20th December 1983:

"But we intervened in a modest way. These have all been very modest transactions; $50 million worth of DM"

Table 1: Qualifications used for Estimation of unpublished Japanese and German Forex Interventions.

Qualifications for Estimated Japanese Forex Interventions, 1973:03-1991:03	Qualifications for Estimated German Forex Interventions, 1973:03-1975:12
Only monthly Absolute Forex Changes greater than $500 million for 1973:3-1977:09	Only monthly Absolute Forex Changes greater than $500 million for 1973:3-1975:12
Only monthly Absolute Forex Changes greater than $1000 million for 1977:10-1991:03	

Figure 2: Estimation of unpublished Monthly German Forex Interventions against the U.S., 1973:3-1975:12, through qualified changes in Germany's Dollar Reserves.

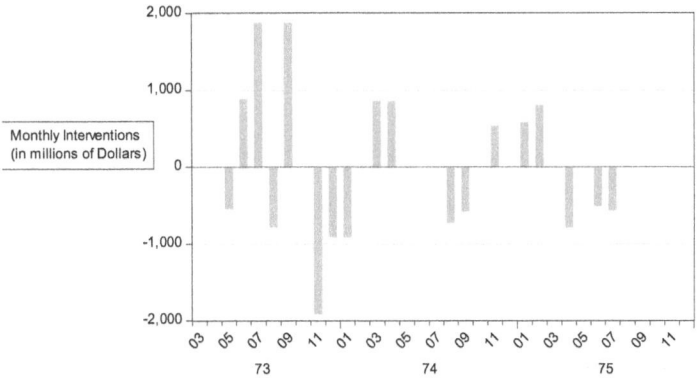

Figure 3: Estimation of unpublished Monthly Japanese Forex Interventions against the U.S., 1973:3-1991:03, through qualified changes in Japan's Dollar Reserves.

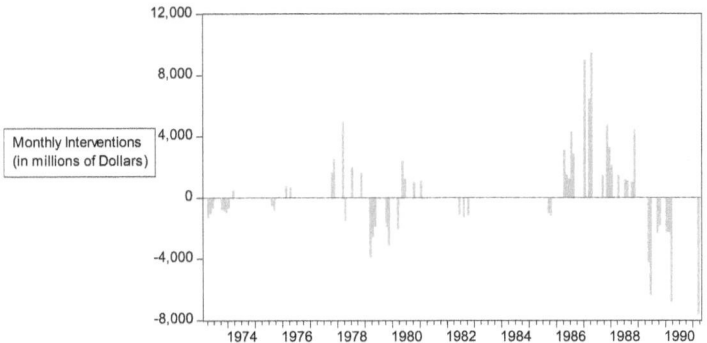

These estimations for Germany chime well with the primary source evidence for German Interventions in 1974 as described in the methodology of the Bundesbank; *Report of the Deutsche Bundesbank*, 1974, pp. 60-61.:

"If the monthly aggregate net reserve movements are taken as a basis, purchases of foreign exchange in 1974 totalled just over DM 8 billion, with sales of foreign exchange amounting to as much as about DM 10 billion"

Reserve estimations for Japan, between 1973:03-1991:03, is an accurate proxy due to the singular pursuit by Japanese policymakers of Yen stabilisation vis-à-vis the Dollar in this crucial period of Japanese economic and political history; and indeed Japanese financial markets were considerably underdeveloped, compared to its economic clout and output, until the late 1980s.

Robustness of my estimations are checked against published results. This will be carried out through the Cross-correlation of estimated against actual published Forex Interventions for Japan, 1991:3-2004:10, and Germany, 1976:1-1990:4. Similar Qualifications are made in Table 2, as were done in Table 1, for the estimates in these periods.

Table 2: Qualifications used for Estimation of published Japanese and German Forex Interventions.

Qualifications for Estimated Japanese Forex Interventions, 1991:3-2004:10	Qualifications for Estimated German Forex Interventions, 1976:1-1990:4
Only monthly Absolute Forex Changes greater than $1000 million for 1991:3-1995:8	Only monthly Absolute Forex Changes greater than $500 million for 1976:1-1990:4
Only monthly Absolute Forex Changes greater than $10000 million for 1995:8-2004:10	

Figure 4: Scatter Plot with red regression line of corresponding Actual and Estimated Monthly Japanese Interventions in millions of Dollars from 1991:3-2004:10.

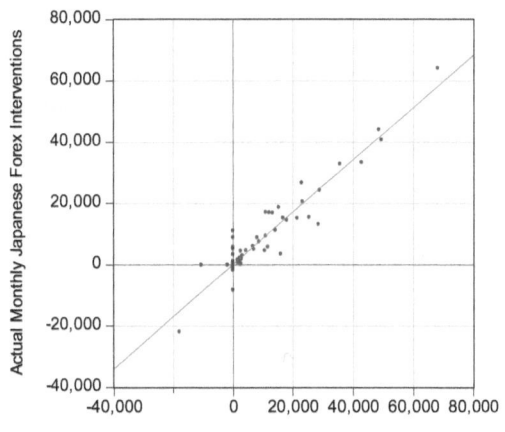

Figure 5: Scatter Plot with red regression line of corresponding Actual and Estimated Monthly German Interventions in millions of Dollars from 1976:1-1991:4.

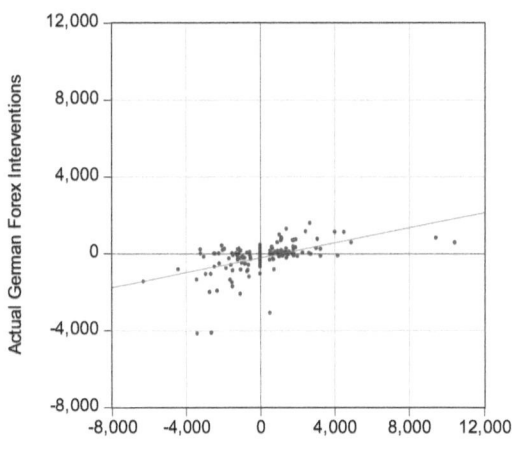

The Robustness analysis from Figures 4 and 5 provides:

Japanese Forex Correlation (Actual, Estimated) = 0.957
German Forex Correlation (Actual, Estimated) = 0.513

For Germany, the correlation is weaker as, following April 1991, increasing focus of the Bundesbank went towards supporting the ERM pegs with the Deutschmark and from early 1990 towards balancing the costs of Reunification through a lax monetary policy; for Japan, the correlation is almost 1 as Eisuke Sakakibara, at the Japanese Ministry of Finance's International Bureau, introduced a new Intervention policy regime following his appointment in mid-1995, consisting of large and infrequent Interventions. Nevertheless, for robustness purposes although these unpublished estimations may not correspond directly to actual changes during those unpublished years, they remain a second best estimation for the purposes of general econometric and economic analysis in this book.

Chapter 2

"Much of our post Bretton Woods structure at the Federal Reserve is an anachronism"

Greenspan

Figure 6: Timeline of Key Events for G-3 Forex Interventions in Post Bretton Woods

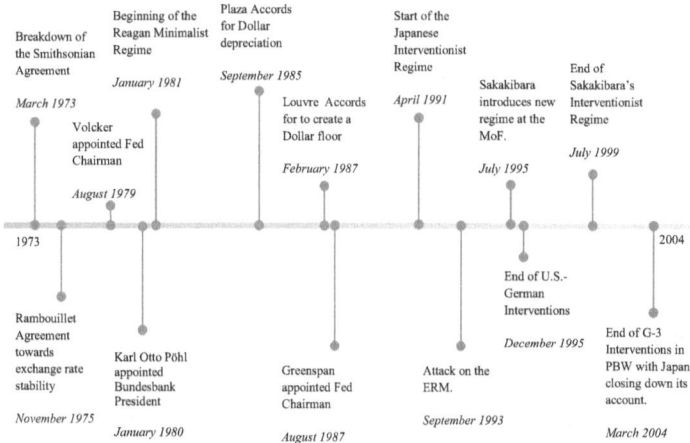

In this Chapter, I expand on the economic history of Forex Interventions in Post Bretton Woods, measured from 1973 till 2004, figure 6 provides a timeline of key Forex Intervention events over this timeline.

Prior to Post Bretton Woods, there were notable British, U.S., and French Interventions in 1927-31 to support the Sterling, Schilling and

Reichsmark, and U.S. Interventions during Bretton Woods in the wake of the Kennedy assassination and the Cuban Missile Crisis. During the fixed exchange rate regime of Bretton Wood centred around the U.S. Dollar, Forex Interventions were conducted by mostly peripheral economies to support their Dollar parities. Under the Bretton Woods system, the U.S. Dollar was the nth currency, in terms of which the, n minus one, other currencies were defined. In theory, the U.S. was responsible for fixing the price of gold at $35 per ounce. However, in practice the U.S. seldom intervened in the Forex or Gold markets; shifting the responsibilities on to other central banks of peripheral economies to fix their parities against the Dollar.

Following Bretton Woods' collapse when the Smithsonian-adjusted Bretton Woods Pegs were finally put down on 12th March 1973, Forex markets became volatile leading to immediate active U.S. and coordinated Forex Interventions, as the intention was observed in the *Federal Reserve Bulletin*, January 1978:

"Joint Intervention by the Treasury, the Federal Reserve, and foreign central banks is designed to check speculation and re-establish order in the foreign exchange markets"

Proponents of flexible exchange rates in Post Bretton Woods felt that the Forex market would provide discipline and coordination, reducing the role of the IMF and replacing the binding rules of Bretton Woods.

Over this period, based on daily interventions, Bordo, Humpage, and Schwartz, have observed in their 2011 paper, 'The Federal Reserve as an informed Foreign-Exchange Trader: 1973-1995', that nearly 74 percent of total U.S. Forex Interventions (measured by days) between

1973 and 1995 occurred between March 1973 and April 1981. Conversely Japanese and German Forex Interventions slowly became more prevalent over Post Bretton Woods.

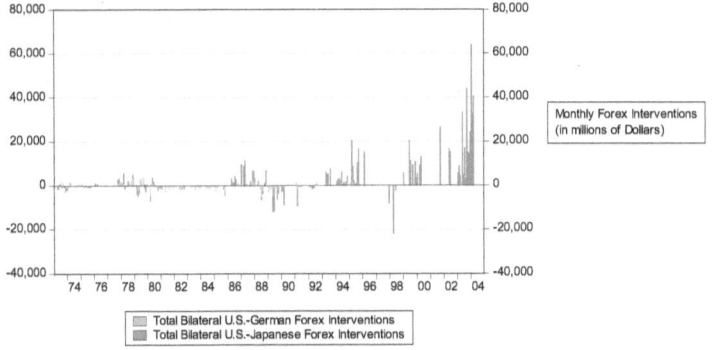

Figure 7: Bilateral Monthly G-3 Forex Interventions in Post Bretton Woods in millions of Dollars, 1973:03-2004:10.

Figure 7 illustrates Bilateral Monthly Interventions, a sum of US-German and US-Japanese Fore Interventions. Following Calculations are made: i) Monthly Interventions are accumulation of Daily Interventions; ii) all non-U.S. Interventions are converted into nominal Dollars by the daily average Yen/Dollar or Deutschmark/Dollar spot rate prevalent on that day, conversion to Dollars in this analysis is justified by primary sources suggesting the Bundesbank and the Japanese Ministry of Finance Intervened solely to influence their currencies' rate with Dollar within liquid Dollar-

Denominated Forex Markets as opposed to Sterling or against each other in Yen or Deutschmark; and iii) positive Interventions on the y-axis are purchases of Dollars whereas negative Interventions denote sales. 'Bilateral Interventions' in this book hereafter refer to pooled Interventions for a currency pair.

Following the Rambouillet agreement, in November 1975, Article IV of the IMF was rewritten to allow members to permanently choose a flexible exchange rate regime. Additionally, the IMF in 1977 provided three guiding principles for Forex Interventions. Firstly, policymakers should not manipulate exchange rates to gain unfair competitiveness; secondly, policymakers should intervene to calm disorderly market conditions; thirdly, policymakers should take into account the interests and the spill-over effects of interventions on others. However, Article IV Section 1 forbids attempts to remedy balance of payments problems by manipulating exchange rates; the section deliberately caters to the proponents of fixed-rates and their fear of Interwar floating-rates. This sentiment was echoed by most published accounts including one in the *Report of the Deutsche Bundesbank*, 1975:

"avoid manipulating exchange rate or the international monetary system in order to prevent the effective balance of payments adjustment or to gain an unfair competitive advantage over other members"

On occasions, the Dollar followed a nominal and real long-term linear trend over Post Bretton Woods; four periods of prominent note are, firstly, the appreciation during the Volcker disinflation period of the early 80s; secondly, the subsequent G-3 coordinated depreciation of the Dollar following the Plaza Accords in 1985. The Plaza Accord was the Group of Five agreement to stop the ongoing appreciation trend of the Dollar; the Louvre Accord signed in 1987 by the Group of Six reversed the prevailing depreciation trend of the Dollar from the Plaza Accord. Finally, an appreciation of the Dollar in the late 90s leading up to the Dotcom bubble and lastly, the depreciation following 2001-07.

The Yen appreciated significantly between 1973 and the mid-1990s from 360 to 80 Yen/ Dollar. Yen appreciation occurred following the Plaza Accord; by late 1988, Japanese policymakers were reluctant for further Yen appreciation, and reduced target interest rates which further fuelled their domestic asset bubble, particularly in property. There were some periods of Yen depreciation between 1995-98, and 2000-03. The Deutschmark was stable in value except noticeable trends in early and late 1980s brought about shift in U.S. exchange rate policies.

U.S. and German Forex Interventions petered out from mid-1995 onwards, whilst Japanese Interventions between 1991 and 2004 were some of the largest and most pronounced in the Economic History of Forex Interventions before coming to an abrupt stop before resuming in September 2010 following the 2008 Financial Crisis.

In Models in this book, I refer to this Japanese regime between 1991 and 2004 as the 'Japanese Interventionist Period'.

For U.S. Forex Interventions, the Fed acted in concert with the U.S. Treasury in conducting U.S. Forex Interventions through the Forex Desk at the New York Fed. Furthermore, the FOMC designated the New York Fed to execute open market transactions on behalf of the Fed and the Treasury held in the System Open Market Account. However, the Gold Reserve Act of 1934 had given the U.S. Treasury prime responsibility for executing on the policy on Forex

Intervention, as was also observed by the then Fed Chairman Alan Greenspan in the *FOMC Transcript*, 3rd November 1987:

"There have been significant disputes over the years as to precisely what the relationship is between the Treasury and the Federal Reserve with respect to the question of exchange rate intervention. As I understand it, even though there are disputable issues here, we largely tend to follow Treasury's lead in this question."

The Gold Reserve Act setup the Exchange Stabilization Fund, whose primary objective was to stabilise the exchange value of the Dollar. Over the course of the last eighty years, the U.S. Treasury in consultation with the Fed has been responsible for coordinating Intervention policy with foreign policymakers as well. However, despite the The Fed never intervening on its own account without the authorisation of the Treasury, subtleties to the relationship between the U.S. Treasury and Fed existed. Greenspan also observed in the *FOMC Transcript*, 29th-30th June 1988,:

"Technically, it's a joint venture. In principle, the interpretation of the Constitution puts the Secretary of the Treasury as essentially speaking for the President--as the quarterback, as you put it. However, in the huddle, so to speak, we get a lot to say. And in many instances we recommend the plays. AndI would think that we've been pretty much on line. In other words, if Sam Cross has a particular point of view--if he likes a specific strategy--more often than not we can convince Treasury that that's appropriate to do and get the authorization."

U.S. Forex Interventions through the Fed are financed from either its portfolio of Forex reserves or via its capacity to borrow via swaps Forex from other central banks and/or the U.S. Treasury. A Swap line is mechanism through which policymakers temporarily exchange domestic and foreign currency, which the borrower pays back on a specified date at the same exchange rate. Warehousing refers to when the Fed undertakes a currency swap transaction, by buying foreign currency on the spot rate and selling it back on a forward rate, with the U.S. Treasury, controversially bypassing the Congressional appropriations process; *FOMC Transcript*, 28th March 1995:

"The only difference when the transaction is done via warehousing is that the usual Congressional appropriations process is circumvented, and the purchase does not show up in the budget....Congress placed the Fed outside the regular appropriations process to protect our independence."

Figure 8: Monthly U.S Forex Intervention in millions of Dollars against Germany and Japan, 1973:03-1995:12, and Nominal and Real Monthly Trade-weighted G-3 Dollar Indices. Additional Information: i) Dollar appreciation registers a decrease in the Index, ii) Monthly Interventions are accumulation of Daily Interventions, and iii) positive Interventions are purchases of Dollars.

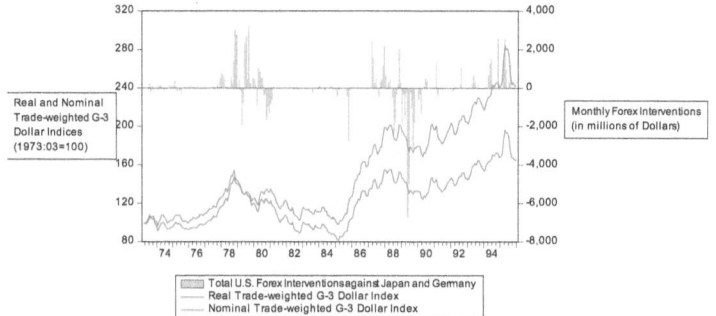

For Figure 8, Adapting the methodology from Loretan, I construct nominal and real Trade-Weighted G-3 Dollar Indices based on German and Japanese trade with the U.S. as constructed below:

$$I_t = I_{t-1} \times (e_{YEN,t}/e_{YEN,t-1})^{w_{JAP,t}} \times (e_{DEM,t}/e_{DEM,t-1})^{w_{GER,t}}$$

$$\Sigma w_t = 1$$

$$w_{JAP,t} = \frac{1}{2}\mu_{JAP,t} + \frac{1}{2}\varepsilon_{JAP,t}, \quad w_{GER,t} = \frac{1}{2}\mu_{GER,t} + \frac{1}{2}\varepsilon_{GER,t}$$

$$\mu_{JAP,t} = M_{JAP,t}/M_{JAP+GER,t}, \quad \mu_{GER,t} = M_{GER,t}/M_{JAP+GER,t}$$

$$\varepsilon_{JAP,t} = X_{JAP,t}/X_{JAP+GER,t}, \quad \varepsilon_{GER,t} = X_{GER,t}/X_{JAP+GER,t}$$

Where $I_t, w_t, \mu_t, \varepsilon_t, e_t, M_t, X_t$ are Index, Weightings, Import Weights, Export Weight, real/nominal exchange rates of Dollar/Deutschmark and Dollar/Yen, U.S. Import Volume, and U.S. Export Volume respectively against Germany and Japan.

Figure 9: Monthly U.S Forex Intervention in millions of Dollars against Japan, 1973:03-2003:10, and Nominal and Real Monthly Dollar/Yen Indices.

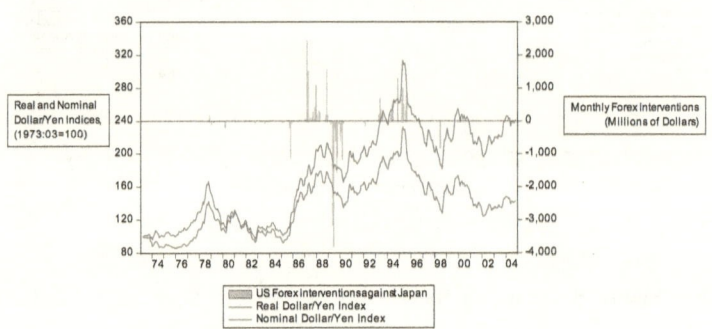

Figure 10: Monthly U.S Forex Intervention in millions of Dollars against Germany, 1973:03-1995:12; and Nominal and Real Monthly Dollar/Deutschmark Indices.

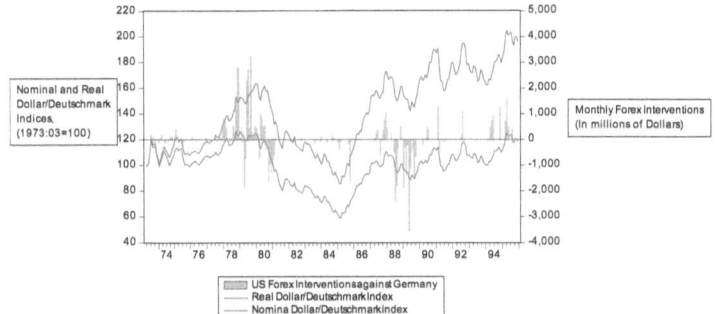

Figure 11: Monthly U.S Forex Intervention in millions of Dollars against Germany and Japan, 1973:03- 2004:10, and % Valuation of the Dollar against the Yen and Deutschmark.

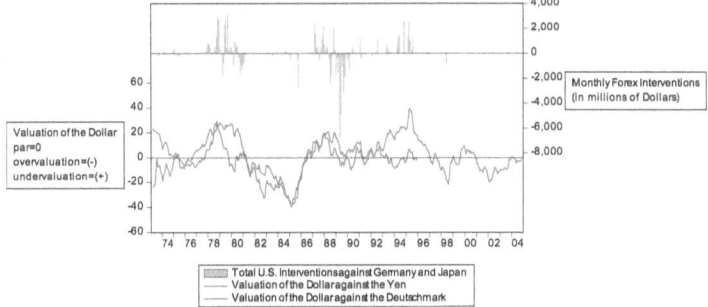

In Figure 11, I estimate the long-run equilibrium Fundamental levels for G-3 currencies from the following methodology:

$$\log(\overline{e}_t) = \delta_0 + \delta_1 t + \delta_2 t^2 + \delta_3 \log\left(\frac{p_t}{p_{j,t}}\right) + \varepsilon_t$$, where e_t is the nominal exchange rate, and p_t are the respective CPI indices. Valuation of the exchange rate is the % logarithmic deviation of actual average monthly spot from the forecasted long-run equilibrium fundamental level of the exchange rate:

$$Valuation_{it} = (\ln e_{it} - \ln \overline{e}_{it}) \times 100$$

Figure 12: Daily U.S. Forex Interventions in millions of Dollars against Japan, Daily Returns on Dollar/Yen, and Daily Volatility of Dollar/Yen, 02/03/1973-29/10/2004. Additional Information: i) Daily Returns are measured by % logarithmic differences of Daily Close Dollar/Yen rate between (t) and (t-1), and ii) Daily Volatilities are the squares of Daily Log Returns.

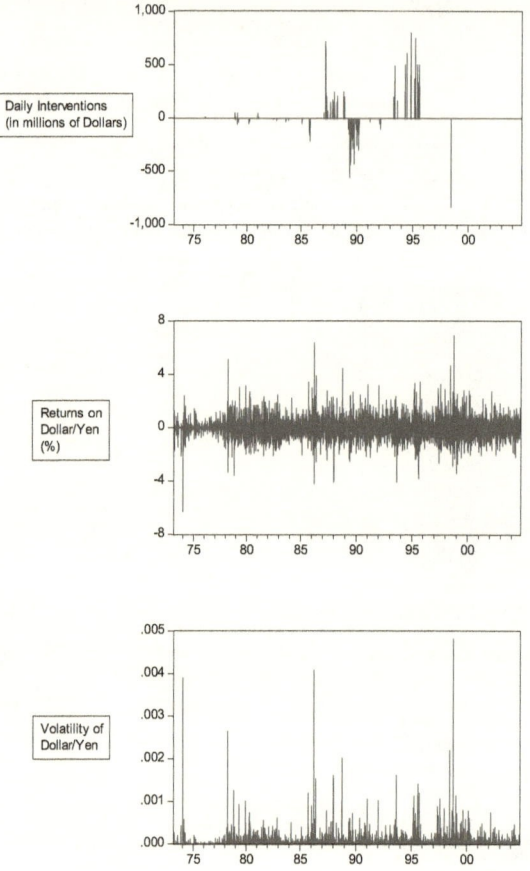

Figure 13: Daily U.S. Forex Interventions in millions of Dollars against Germany, Daily Returns on Dollar/Deutschmark, and Daily Volatility of Dollar/Deutschmark, 02/03/1973-29/12/1995. Additional Information: i) Daily Returns are measured by % logarithmic difference of Daily Close Dollar/Deutschmark rate between (t) and (t-1), and ii) Daily Volatilities are the squares of Daily Log Returns.

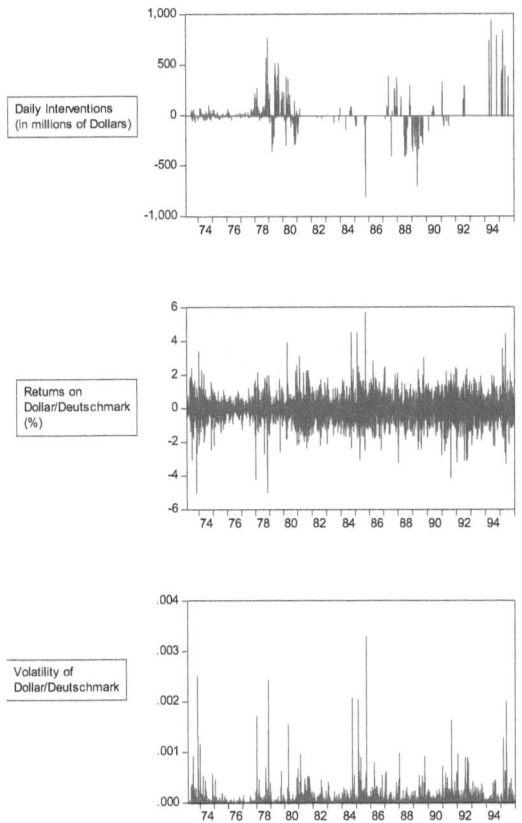

The U.S. intervened four times as often against the Deutschmark then against the Yen between 1973 and 1995. U.S. Interventions against the Deutschmark were more evenly distributed between purchases and sales; in comparison, sixty percent of U.S. Interventions against the Yen consisted of purchases, suggesting U.S. policymakers were more concerned of Dollar overvaluation and/or Yen undervaluation.

Daily U.S. Forex Interventions against the Deutschmark between 1973 and 1997 were on average $80 million, with a median of $31 million. Similarly, Daily U.S. Forex Intervention against the Yen averaged $131 million with a median at $90 million. Bordo, Humpage, and Schwartz argue the largest U.S. Forex Intervention of $950 and $800 million against the Deutschmark and Yen, respectively, were inefficiently large; based on their probit analyses the reported estimates suggests interventions of $300 and $400 million were sufficient to guarantee success against the Deutschmark and Yen, respectively.

In the early days of Post Bretton Woods, U.S. Forex Interventions were small and frequent; a consequence of Dollar volatility and depreciation which arose through unchecked U.S. Monetary Policy and the Fed's failure to pursue price stability under 'Stagflationary' circumstances in the 1970s. U.S. inflation accelerated to 12% in 1974 due to worsening inflation expectations and loss of monetary credibility. Additionally, the Keynesian economic framework of early Post Bretton Woods had a policy preference for low unemployment over inflation; Orphanides found, in '*Monetary-Policy Rules and the Great Inflation*', the coefficient on the unemployment was greater than the inflation term in an estimated Taylor rule for early Post Bretton Woods period. Furthermore, an underestimation of the natural rate of unemployment existed and a strong belief in the short-run Philips trade-off, led to U.S. macro-management taking the form of stop-go policies.

Table 3: List of Fed Chairmen, and corresponding U.S. Treasury Secretaries and Presidents, 1973-2001.

Fed Chairmen	Treasury Secretaries	Presidents
Arthur Burns (February 1970-March 1978)	George Shultz (June 1972-May 1974)	Richard Nixon (January 1969-August 1974)
	William Simon (May 1974-January 1977)	Gerald Ford (August 1974-January 1977)
	Michael Blumenthal (January 1977-August 1979)	Jimmy Carter (January 1977-January 1981)
William Miller (March 1978-August 1979)	Michael Blumenthal (January 1977-August 1979)	Jimmy Carter (January 1977-January 1981)

Paul Volcker	William Miller	Jimmy Carter
(August 1979-August 1987)	(August 1979-January 1981)	(January 1977-January 1981)
	Donald Regan	Ronald Reagan
	(January 1981-February 1985)	(January 1981-January 1989)
	James Baker	
	(February 1985-August 1988)	
Alan Greenspan	James Baker	Ronald Reagan
(August 1987-January 2006)	(February 1985-August 1988)	(January 1981-January 1989)
	Peter McPherson	George H.W. Bush
	(August 1988-September 1988)	(January 1989-January 1993)
	Nicholas Brady	Bill Clinton
	(September 1988-January 1993)	(January 1993-January 2001)
	Lloyd Bentsen	
	(January 1993-December 1994)	
	Frank Newman	
	(December 1994-January	

1995)
Robert Rubin
(January 1995-July 1999)
Lawrence Summers
(July 1999-January 2001)

At the initiative of the Burns and Miller Fed between 1970-79, the Desk at the New York Fed conducted Forex Interventions in the 1970s mostly through borrowing from swap lines; which were quickly and secretly repaid to minimise influence on "market psychology"; as described in the *FOMC Memorandum of Discussion*, 15th July 1975:

"...several techniques were being used to acquire foreign currencies for the same purpose--that of repaying drawings on the swap lines. Mr. Pardee [Deputy Manager for Foreign Operations] added that when the Desk was acquiring currencies to repay debt, it tried to avoid having any noticeable influence on the market...Chairman Burns asked why it was advantageous to conceal the fact that the System was purchasing German marks through the BIS. Mr. Pardee replied that the market was generally aware that the System had a substantial debt denominated in German marks and would react upon learning that the System was acquiring marks through market purchases. In the process of repaying debt, it was preferable to avoid exerting such an influence on the market."

Interventions were small during the Burns-Miller Fed due to the Desk's small portfolio of foreign exchange and Closed because of the early fear of market speculation against the intervention's success. Private agents were aware of the reserve-thin vulnerability of U.S.

Forex Interventions; swap arrangements required the consent and conditionality of foreign central banks, in particular the Bundesbank, and perceived unwillingness of the latter to act to support the Dollar deleteriously influenced market psychology.

Following the collapse of Bretton Woods, the view of the Fed was that the exchange markets required perennial guidance and order as well as coordinated control from all policy levers. *FOMC Memorandum of Discussion*, 9th July 1973:

"Chairman [Burns] commented that the present situation was one in which speculators, having no confidence in currencies or governments, were moving from one currency to another. Perhaps such a situation could be said to reflect "market forces," but it could also be described as chaotic. The purpose of intervention would be to restore some order to the market...there also was support for the observation that the recent experience with floating exchange rates had not been a very happy one...The Chairman said he would agree that little long-run gain could be expected from intervention unless it were accompanied by effective measures in the area of domestic economic and financial policy."

And *FOMC Memorandum of Discussion*, November 19th 1973:

"Although the dollar has fallen back a bit from its peak, the markets have remained orderly and thus far there has been no need for support operations. Obviously, the situation calls for close watching; if there were a sharp break, the case for intervention might be very strong."

Initially, U.S. Intervention policy took a conservative stance in early 1973; there was also a belief that prolonged and continuous interventions may prevent the effective functioning of the recently floating Dollar; *FOMC Memorandum of Discussion*, 20th March 1973:

"...there was always the possibility that intervention would be carried to the point of preventing the system of floating rates from functioning effectively. Central banks should not be poised to intervene at some slight provocation; official operations should be reserved for dealing with undue gyrations in rates. Chairman Burns agreed. He added that among the central bankers meeting in Paris there was a widespread--although not necessarily universal--feeling that there ought to be little or no intervention for a time."

The interventionist policy mind-set was immediately evident following the Rambouillet agreement, in November 1975, leading to successive U.S. Forex Interventions. Despite the counter-efforts of the Bundesbank to slow things down as outlined in the *Report of the Deutsche Bundesbank*, 1975:

"The participants [at the Rambouillet agreement] affirmed their intention to work for greater stability in exchange rate relations. At the same time it was stated explicitly that "this involves efforts to restore greater stability in underlying economic and financial conditions"...This wording recognises a point of view long maintained by Germany...The implementation of the Rambouillet agreement on stabilising interventions in the exchange market is to be ensured by occasional consultations between the finance ministers of the countries concerned"

On the other hand, by 1977-1978, U.S. policymakers allowed the Dollar to depreciate in order "to correct the external disequilibrium". However, following 1978, policy perception of a continued decline was judged as unnecessary given macro conditions as outlined in the *Economic Report of the President*, January 1979:

"...some of the earlier 1977-78 dollar decline had been necessary to correct the external disequilibrium, the continued decline of the dollar had become disorderly and was not justified by fundamental economic conditions."

U.S. policymakers realised uncertainty over the Dollar's future equilibrium, current account deficit, and inflationary pressures in the U.S. causally affected Dollar volatility.

During the Burns-Miller Fed, Interventions were made to check rapid depreciations of the Dollar, especially between January and March 1975 when there were successful coordinated Interventions placed against the Deutschmark. *The Economist*, in 22nd November 1975, questioned the ability of sustained U.S. Interventions following the Rambouillet agreement without the use of swap facilities or short-term credit, especially due to a small U.S. reserve position of $16 billion. Nevertheless, Policymakers felt the daily variability in exchange rates between 1974 and 1977 was attributed to a lessening of external shocks.

Additionally the Desk placed orders through the agency of a commercial bank in the New York Brokers' Market; this allowed the Desk to conduct Open and Closed Interventions, thereby cleverly channelling private speculation and signalling information. Policymakers were occasionally sceptical over the institutional construct of Closed Interventions, which led to informational advantage to the Desk's proxy Banks, as later asked by Chairman Greenspan in the *FOMC Transcript*, 5th-6th July 1989, when the Fed started using more than one commercial bank to place orders by the late 1980s:

"CHAIRMAN GREENSPAN: I believe Governor Angell was raising the question as to whether the individual bank trades on that [Forex Intervention] information, which is not available to other participants in the market.

MR. CROSS: Well, in a sense, a bank can do that any time we are in the market and are trading with a bank. As I say, if we are operating quite openly we might go out and talk to 5 banks or 10 banks. They might choose to join us, and this helps move the market in the direction [we want] if they're convinced that it's going that way. We do move around from one institution to another; we don't use the same one, obviously. Sometimes we might use several at once, but we do it in a way that they are not supposed to go tell all their customers and others that they are operating on behalf of the Fed."

The Desk sometimes coordinated Interventions with other lesser central banks to stem any spillover effects of interventions against the Deutschmark and/or Yen. For instance, by the mid-1980s, the Desk sold Deutschmarks, but also sold French Francs to avoid aggravating the perceived weakness of the former to the latter within the European Monetary System, as accounted by the *Federal Reserve Bulletin*, June 1980:

"From April 8 through 10 [th 1980] the dollar dropped sharply across the board, declining about 5 percent against the major European currencies in only 24 hours. To cushion the decline, the Trading Desk intervened in sizable amounts, operating in German marks and Swiss francs. The Desk also sold French francs, in consultation with the Bank of France, to avoid aggravating the weakness of the mark relative to the franc within the EMS."

Overall, Intervention success in early Post Bretton Woods was undermined by the 'Great Inflation' and policy inaction to address worsening macroeconomic conditions; this was recognised by 1978 in FOMC meetings and U.S. economic reports, increasingly by the soon to be Chairman Paul Volcker; *FOMC Transcript*, 5th January 1978:

"VICE CHAIRMAN VOLCKER: May I inject just one other thought, Mr. Chairman [Burns]? I think the success of this whole [Forex Intervention] operation is not going to hinge on intervention entirely in the short run, *although that's the motivation for the immediate change. I think all those things that we worried about before--oil and even domestic monetary policy--are very relevant here and I don't think we ought to lose sight of that*

CHAIRMAN BURNS. I want to endorse that completely. Actually, our [Forex] intervention so far has demonstrated to my mind the futility of the exercise pretty much. Now, we are getting some psychological benefit out of the recent announcement and I hope it lasts. We are intervening more actively and I think we should up to a point, but I don't want to see this overdone."

Chairman Burns commented furthermore on the relationship between Forex Interventions and perceived complacency displayed by other Federal Institutions, leading to perceived government policy failures, in the *FOMC Transcript*, 28th February 1978:

"I'll make a comment now which previously, under normal conditions, I would have delayed making. But in making this comment, I must advise the Committee once again that everything that is said in this room at all times must be treated on an absolutely confidential basis. There are differences within the government about steps that can and should be taken to deal with the dollar problem. The more active our [Forex] intervention is, the more excuse others within this government have for not taking some of the more fundamental steps that need to be taken to restore the integrity of the dollar in foreign exchange markets. That is a political consideration of the very greatest importance and one that I think we should very much keep in mind...Namely, [we should do so] to maintain a certain element of pressure on others in the government to the effect that this intervention activity is of ephemeral, transitory significance and that other steps that can be taken should be taken without further delay."

Private agents during this period also doubted U.S. policymakers' intent to deal effectively with accelerating inflation. U.S. Interventions were made in the perceived belief of mitigating a depreciating Dollar from further adding inflationary pressure or in 'buying time' for remedial policy action. Greene argues, in '*U.S. Experience with Exchange Market Intervention: September 1977-December 1979*', without corresponding measures to address the fundamental weaknesses of the causes of the Dollar Depreciation, that Intervention had little effect.

Between 1977 and 1981, relative inflationary pressures in the U.S. versus other advanced economies significantly depreciated the Dollar against the Deutschmark and Yen; leading to a series of coordinated Interventions starting in November 1978 designed to correct the excessive exchange rate movements. 'Carter Bonds' were issued, in DEM 5.5 Billion from Germany, with an additional CHF 2.5 Billion from Switzerland, between 1978-1979 by the U.S. Treasury along with Deutschmark Swap lines of $6B to mitigate the fall of the Dollar during the Carter Administration as recorded by *the Monthly Report of the Deutsche Bundesbank*, December 1979:

"U.S. monetary authorities obtained the Deutschmark [for Intervention] by drawing both on the swap line [...and] issuing DM-denominated bearer Treasury Notes in the German capital market"

The Carter Bonds served to close the gap in the "war chest theory" of Interventions, which is the theory that interventions should be backed by hard reserves rather than other forms, including swap lines. This was reiterated in the:

"But I do think we should keep in mind that as recently as 1977 or 1978...when the perception was that the United States was going in the tank, the United States government, including the Federal Reserve, found it necessary to approach the world at large, hat in hand, and establish what was then a $30 billion war chest. To be sure, a lot of that war chest was

smoke and mirrors and some of it was subsequently financed as you pointed out through the so-called Carter bonds."

Greene suggests furthermore U.S. policymakers initially aimed to smooth exchange rate volatility as opposed to influence its direction in early Post Bretton Woods. Estimates of the Forex Intervention reaction function, carried out by Bordo, Humpage, and Schwartz, also report a priority given to smoothing exchange rate movements in order to "lean-against-the-wind". According to Bordo, Humpage, and Schwartz, their second criterion in *'The Federal Reserve as an informed Foreign-Exchange Trader: 1973-1995'*, U.S. Forex Interventions were more successful between 1973 and 1995. They had measured their second criterion as:

"Our second success criterion scores an intervention as a success if the United States sells foreign exchange and the dollar continues to depreciate but does so by less than over the previous day. Likewise, this criterion counts intervention as a success if the United States buys foreign exchange and the dollar continues to appreciate but does so by less than over the previous day"

Unlike the first and third criteria, success of Forex Interventions measured by the second criterion reported no same-day negative forecast value of exchange rate. Where their first and third criterion respectively is:

"[first] success criterion counts an official U.S. sale or purchase of foreign exchange on a particular day as a success if the dollar appreciates or depreciates, as the case may be, over that same day...Our general [third] success criterion incorporates SC1 [first Criterion] and SC2 [second Criterion]. Accordingly, an intervention sale of foreign exchange on a particular day is successful if the dollar appreciates or if it depreciates by less than on the previous day."

By 1979, the newly-appointed Volcker Fed had qualms over unilateral Forex Interventions, as outlined at the very beginning of his term in the *FOMC Transcript*, 17th July 1979:

"The market has had enough experience with intervention alone that it gets to the point where one wonders whether it's helpful or harmful in some circumstances, particularly against the background where the Bundesbank may well get very restive very soon about the amounts of liquidity we're creating in their markets."

Volcker's assessment of earlier interventions was also somewhat negative as accounted by him, prior to his tenure as Fed Chairman in 1975 in *'Priorities for the International Monetary System'*:

"In other words, intervention is a tactic—sometimes useful, sometimes not. By itself, it will accomplish little if not accompanied by appropriate domestic policies, by internal stability, and by some willingness to take account of international considerations in policymaking. Floating rates are attractive precisely because they give us a beneficial new degree of freedom in reconciling our domestic policies with open international markets. But to act as though nations can have complete independence in national policy in an interdependent world would be to abuse the system. The result would be to diminish the chances for greater stability in exchange markets."

Volcker also took a different approach to monetary policy and interventions compared to his predecessors, in particular Burns; implicit in the early FOMC Transcripts of early Post Bretton Woods is the differing economic beliefs of Burns and Volcker. In Volcker and Gyohten, *Changing Fortunes, The World's Money and the Threat to American Leadership*, Volcker at times voiced his disappointment at the lack of collegiate coordination of Intervention and Monetary Policy in the Burns' Fed. However, similar to Burns Fed, the Volcker

Fed continued to believe in the perceived impact of Interventions on "market psychology", *FOMC Transcript*, 29th-30th March 1982:

"Well, they [the market] seem to feel that if there is a coordinated effort, it will have considerably more effect in modifying the market psychology and in indicating that there will be a sustained effort to keep the rates from moving too strongly in the direction they're now moving."

Under the first term of the Reagan Administration a minimalist strategy was taken towards U.S. Interventions. Volcker and Gyohten attributed this policy shift to Reagan's new Treasury Secretary, Don Regan. The U.S. Treasury implemented this 'minimal' Interventionist policy based on Intervening "only when necessary to counter conditions of disorder in the market".

Due to this factor, namely, the belief the Dollar should be determined by market forces, and also because of Volcker Disinflation, the Dollar appreciated by over 40 percent between 1981 and 1985 against the Deutschmark and Yen; U.S. policymakers rarely intervened in this period and questioned the effectiveness of Interventions. Other policymakers also questioned the effectiveness of their Interventions against the U.S., *Report of the Deutsche Bundesbank*, 1981:

"The fact that it was not possible to calm the foreign exchange markets durably, despite the considerable volume of interventions, is probably due to the abstention of the United States from intervention operations; without its active participation, dollar interventions appear to be less convincing to the market and are therefore not so effective"

The Volcker Fed also expressed dissatisfaction of shared Intervention policy with the U.S. Treasury, leading to less reactive and more political Interventions, *FOMC Transcript*, 28th-29th March 1983:

"VICE CHAIRMAN SOLOMON: Under what circumstances would you encourage the foreign exchange Desk, Mr. Chairman, to make to you and the Treasury a recommendation that intervention seems appropriate to us? Earlier we made that recommendation a few times when there had been a very substantial weakening in a key foreign currency and the Treasury would then say: Well, let's wait a while and watch. And so the opportunity would be missed. [Their] reaction might have been that if there's a further weakening, yes, we'll do something. But by then there had already been a 1 percent or a 1/2 percent move and then there wasn't any further weakening.

CHAIRMAN VOLCKER. That has been the story of our life recently. It moves and we're ready and then it moves the other way."

Volcker and Gyohten also recount, in particular, when "*Mrs. Thatcher telephoned President Reagan [...] to urge intervention in support of the pound sterling [as the Dollar was hitting the sacred barrier of one-to-one]. However ideologically reluctant [...] this request it could not reject*".

The appreciation of the Dollar in the earlier 1980s was attributed to the "*strong U.S. economy, large budget deficit, tight monetary policy, and high [relative] real interest rates*" as recounted by Jacobson in 'U.S. Foreign Exchange Operations'. In Reagan's first term, U.S. policymakers believed Interventions could not ensure the smooth functioning of an International Monetary System which depends fundamentally on sound economic and financial policies.

By 1985, protectionist lobbies spurred U.S. Congressional Committees to consider making independent Congressional Forex Interventions, thereby threatening to undermine the policy space of the Fed and Treasury. This led to policy measures under Reagan's second term Treasury Secretary, James Baker, to correct the exchange rate level and initiate collective G-3 exchange rate coordination. Volcker was receptive towards the policy change intending to accommodate a compatible monetary policy towards it.

Much of the groundwork for the subsequent Plaza Accord was laid in diplomatic exchanges between Japanese and U.S. economic policymakers in the summer of 1985. Volcker and Gyohten write that the then Japanese Finance minister, Noboru Takeshita, needing prior explicit approval from the Diet for global policy coordination, went for a round of Golf besides Narita Airport only to sneak out on Pan Am to New York to start discreet meetings leading up to the Accords, thus also avoiding the hordes of Japanese corporates who took Jap Air for transpacific travel. Up to 1985, U.S. Interventions against the Yen were rare and, moreover, unsuccessful in affecting the bilateral exchange rate.

Following Plaza, coordinated Forex Interventions were held by the G-3 Economies, France, and Britain; collectively known as the G-5 Economies. By 1987 the group was further expanded to Canada and Italy, and became known as the Group of Seven, G-7 Economies. Nevertheless the G-3 economies underwrote global economic policy, and more so, were the primary Forex Interveners during the first thirty years of Post-Bretton Woods. These initial post-Plaza Interventions led to the depreciation of the Dollar; also, Interventions became more Open and worked through the signalling mechanism.

There was no word on Intervention in the actual Plaza Communique, however following the signing of the Accord a statement was produced to initiate the signalling mechanism. However this was not sufficient for some G-5 Plaza participants believing the Dollar would continue to rise further. But all participants agreed on an

Intervention Strategy but kept it secret in order to prevent "wild speculation"; G-5 meetings prior to Plaza were always kept secret. Volcker and Gyohten regales how the Japanese Prime minister served as the acting Finance Minister to allow for the actual Finance Minister, who would otherwise need to seek approval from the Diet and cabinet to leave the country, to attend the meeting prior to and during the Plaza Accords.

Seven days following Plaza, from 23rd September to 1st October 1985, the G-5 economies sold $2.7 billion, against the U.S., of which Japan intervened with $1.25 billion; six weeks, later a total of $10.2 billion Forex Interventions against the Dollar were made. Additionally, *FOMC Transcript*, 16th-17th December 1985, reporting "since September 22, all the G-10 countries together have spent around $13-$14 billion [intervening against the Dollar]".

The concurrent G-5 announcements on Interventions caught Forex markets by surprise in the Autumn of 1985; *Federal Reserve Bulletin*, February 1986:

"The G-5 [Plaza] announcement had an immediate and strong effect on dollar exchange rates. In part, the exchange market reaction reflected the fact that the announcement was unexpected. More importantly, market participants noted that the initiative had come from the United States and viewed it as a change in the U.S. government's previously perceived attitude of accepting or even welcoming the strong dollar."

Obstfeld, in *'The Effectiveness of Foreign-Exchange Intervention: Recent Experience'*, concluded the shift in monetary and fiscal policy were the main policy factors determining exchange rate realignment following Plaza. Relative real and nominal interest rate spreads between the U.S., and Germany and Japan reinforced Dollar

Depreciation following Plaza as well as expectations thereof, *Federal Reserve Bulletin*, May 1986:

"The G-5 [Plaza] agreement was interpreted by market participants as reducing the likelihood that the Federal Reserve would tighten reserve conditions. Many market participants expected the U.S. authorities to act to lower U.S. interest rates, either in concert with other G-5 countries or alone, to reduce the incentive to invest in dollar-denominated assets and thereby encourage an appreciation of nondollar currencies."

However, as reiterated by Cross in '*Treasury and Federal Reserve Foreign Exchange Operations*', following post-Plaza, G-3 Policymakers publically denied there existed any agreement towards coordination of interest rate spreads to favour Dollar depreciation.

The G-6 Communique, of 22nd February 1987, was signed 15 months after Plaza Communique, to "foster stability of exchange rates around current [fundamental] levels" following the reduction of "external imbalances" since Plaza. Private agents were also sceptical by then given the deteriorating economic indicators that "the [U.S] authorities would attach a high enough priority to exchange rate stability to alter domestic economic policies if necessary" (*Federal Reserve Bulletin*, October 1987).

The dissonance of Policy coordination between the Fed and the Treasury was evident when, by late 1987, Interventions were "draining reserve" whilst the Fed was "adding reserves to add liquidity". Alan Greenspan replaced Volcker as Fed Chairman in 1987, Greenspan shared the minimalist market philosophy of the Reagan Administration and interpreted the Fed's role as "junior partners" to the Treasury; *FOMC Transcript*, 3rd November 1987:

"There have been significant disputes over the years as to precisely what the relationship is between the Treasury and the Federal Reserve with respect to the question of exchange rate intervention. As I understand it, even though there are disputable issues here, we largely tend to follow Treasury's lead in this question. The Treasury's position, while basically favorable to the Louvre [Accord] as a general procedure, is that they nonetheless are interested in making certain that we don't endeavor to defend a particular position which is indefensible. And, I would think that while the general view of the [Treasury] Secretary sort of backed and filled on various occasions, ideally, he would like to see the markets stabilize on their own without any actions on our part, whether through monetary or intervention policies."

But the Greenspan Fed continued to Intervene, in the spirit of cooperation created by Plaza and Louvre, "to show the flag", *FOMC Transcript*, 26th March 1991:

"in late '87 and early '88: The discussion around the table at that time, as I recall it, was that there was some sense of agreement in some parts of this [FOMC] body that in large open economies sterilized intervention does not impact exchange rates over time and that, therefore, intervention is nothing but churning and noise to the market and it can interfere with our policy efforts. At that time the argument was--and I think it was an appropriate argument--that we ought to have some [foreign currency balances] at least for cooperation purposes, to show the flag and to be part of this process."

However, members of the FOMC expressed disenchantment at further Interventions by 1989. Members also felt further cooperation with the Treasury on Interventions was undermining the Fed; best displayed by Governor Wayne Angell, *FOMC Transcript*, 5th-6th July 1989:

"I just don't hold that these kinds of [intervention] moves make that much difference. But even if they did, I do not believe it's appropriate for a

government agency in a market society to be acting in such a manner. It's not appropriate for us; I believe it opens up the possibility for the charge of someone privately benefitting from what we do."

Members also felt further cooperation with the Treasury on Interventions was undermining the Fed. Leading to at times acrimonious exchanges between FOMC members, but most prominently recorded on 3rd October 1989 in the then FOMC Transcripts. These discussions were more important in light of the concerted sales of Yen and Deutschmark throughout 1989, in particular between 1989:05 and 1989:10, U.S. Forex Interventions against Japan and Germany amounted to around $18 billion. In light of the incompatibility of a weak dollar with a reactive and contractionary monetary policy aiming towards price stability, objections over conflicts between price and exchange rate stability were offered during the same exchanges, *FOMC Transcript*, 3rd October 1989:

"I don't believe the way to get the dollar down is to bomb it through intervention. I think the best way to do it is to deal with it in a monetary policy way...But we can't have that commitment to price level stability without having a strong dollar. That is, a strong commitment to price level stability [requires appropriate] interest rate differentials and the dollar remaining strong."

U.S Interventions in the form of sales of Dollars, by mid-1988 and early 1989, were inconsistent with the then contractionary monetary policy and implicit price targets. Following October 1989, U.S. Forex Interventions petered off despite a series of concerted Treasury-led Interventions in the spring of 1990. But given the policy trade-offs, the discussion came to a headwind in the FOMC meeting on 27th March 1990; in the year leading up to which U.S. Interventions totalled $24 billion. Greenspan corralled the discussion, during the meeting, towards an increase in the authorization for Forex Interventions and warehousing, however three members explicitly dissented; an unusual occurrence in the Greenspan Fed.

By the G-7 meeting in April 1990 the Treasury expressed its lack of confidence in Interventions, as recounted by Greenspan in *FOMC Transcript*, 11th April 1990:

"First of all, what was really quite interesting as we went into [the G7 Meeting] was the increasingly anti-intervention views of our Secretary of the Treasury. It became clear when the Secretary was on his way to Los Angeles to meet with Mr. Hashimoto [the Japanese Minister of Finance] a week or so ago that he was already beginning to abandon support for very strong intervention, essentially on the grounds--as he in fact indicated to the G-7-- that he had come into the process with what he called an open mind but had been observing the phenomenon now for quite a while and had concluded in far stronger language than anyone on this Committee has that 'It just doesn't work'."

The amount warehoused by the Treasury at the Fed decreased in 1990 from $9 to $2.5 billion. Unlike in early Fed Regimes in Post-Bretton Woods, G-3 Forex holdings of the Treasury and the Fed were quite significant, amounting to $30 billion and $18 billion in Deutschmarks and Yen, respectively. Nevertheless, Greenspan had come to understand the Fed's monetary objectives would gradually supersede exchange rate policy in the 1990s, leaving the latter for the Treasury's purview as was slowly conceded by Greenspan, serving as a stated indictment against Interventions, in *FOMC Transcript*, 18th August 1992:

"This issue is pretty clear legally. The President of the United States and through him the Secretary of the Treasury--who if push came to shove statutorily could demand that we do certain things, not necessarily with our portfolio but on their behalf--is in charge. There's an ambiguity in the law with respect to whether we could act independently. I suspect that we could find a lawyer in this city who would say that we could buy deutschemarks while the Treasury is selling them. The operations have evolved over the years as a joint venture between the Treasury and the Federal Open Market Committee. Sometimes it has worked well; sometimes it has worked less than well"

By 1994, despite pressures from the media, markets, and Treasury to support the April-May 1994 U.S. Interventions through a change in the Fed's monetary policy, Greenspan condoned the Treasury's actions in May 1994, feeling this would be part and parcel of separating exchange rate from monetary objectives; *FOMC Transcript*, 5-6th of July 1994:

"You know, it depends really on whether we expect markets to be wholly efficient and not run periodically into some significant abnormalities that an intervention could rebalance. This is the key question. You are telling me that we should not respond to this market at all; it's the Treasury which has to be convinced of that, which they were not... In all of these actions it has been we who have fended off recommended interventions which we thought were superfluous and potentially counterproductive. We have only gone forward when we thought there was at least a reasonable shot."

By the end of 1994, monetary and exchange rate conflicts were leading to some FOMC members thinking of the "credibility" with which the Fed relies on to justify its monetary independence, best summarised by the exchange between Alfred Broaddus, who was president of the Richmond Fed, and Greenspan, *FOMC Transcript*, 15th of November 1994:

"MR. BROADDUS: I wonder if I could put another alternative on the table--that we not intervene at all. I realize that there are many people on the Committee who would disagree with that because they think that, at least in a limited way, intervention may be useful from time to time, and I certainly respect those views. But I have to tell you that I personally have very serious reservations about the wisdom of our continuing to intervene...As you said, Mr. Chairman, it is now widely agreed that sterilized intervention doesn't have any sustained impact on exchange rates unless it sends a signal that we are going to follow it up with a monetary policy action. This implies, for me at least, and this is really the heart of the matter, that it is not really possible for the Fed to maintain a truly independent monetary policy for an extended period of time while following the Treasury's lead on foreign exchange policy. Now, of course, in reality the way I see this is that we have maintained our independence by not making a commitment to follow interventions with monetary policy actions. But that's not a perfect situation either. I think it is a problem because of the possibility that these operations will not be successful. Of course, back in June we had an operation I think most people would agree was not successful. That really bothers me from the standpoint of credibility because when we participate in an operation like this and it is not successful, we get associated with that result. Specifically, we lose credibility. It is adverse for us from the standpoint of public perceptions about the central bank and what we can do. I think that can reduce our effectiveness over time in conducting monetary policy generally. It is an important issue; it is a broad issue. Again, I would respectfully submit that we ought to consider withdrawing from these kinds of operations, maybe not immediately but gradually in some way. This is a side point: If we did that, we would not need swap arrangements. Frankly, I would oppose renewing the swap arrangements this morning. Let me say that I am not opposed to or saying that the U.S. Government should never intervene in foreign exchange markets. I am simply saying that I don't think we should participate except perhaps as the Treasury's agent.

CHAIRMAN GREENSPAN: You are raising an interesting question. The dilemma we have is that if we withdraw and act strictly as an agent, we then *lose any voice in altering or casting the structure of the policy that they would like to implement. The points you are making, Al[fred], are quite to the point; I don't disagree with that. The question that we have to trade off here is, do we wish to remove ourselves from any influence on how these things are done? In my experience, because we are involved in the discussions, we have headed off a lot of actions that I think would have been detrimental, more so than what we have done. There is unquestionably the problem that we are not the final voice on that; legally they are. Nonetheless, we do have a de facto veto if we wish to use it, and the reason we do is because we participate in those discussions. We have to choose whether we want to lose what is in my judgment a very valuable asset in tempering what the Treasury Department does. It is not a simple tradeoff."*

There was a steady evolution of Intervention and Monetary Economic Policy in the 1980s; under Reagan's first term there was a severe lack of coordination of macroeconomic policies between the G-3 economies. Volcker and Gyohten consider Treasury Secretary James Baker and his deputy, Richard Darman, as instrumental in using the G-5 as a means towards global policy coordination. The U.S. pursued a lax fiscal policy despite having a large budget deficit, whilst Japan and Germany maintained stringent fiscal prudence despite large trade surpluses, creating global imbalances in Post-Bretton Woods reflected in a rising Dollar.

Arguably, Plaza-Louvre hallmarked the beginnings of attempted corrections to these Global Imbalances in Post-Bretton Woods. The Plaza and Louvre accords were meant to address this imbalance but did not produce the immediate adjustment in the balance of payments which Policymakers desired; much later did it came to the realisation of Policymakers that exchange rate correction would not eliminate the yield arbitrage between U.S. and non-U.S. assets thus allowing the U.S. to maintain a trade deficit and positive net-investment position.

From 1988 onwards focus shifted towards microeconomic structural policies to address some of the failures of coordinated macroeconomic policies. Similarly, U.S. policymakers took into account private agent sentiments which in turn reacted to forex-related news events such as conflagrations in the Middle East affecting Oil prices, provisional releases of employment and output results of the previous quarter, and fiscal deficits. U.S. policymakers ultimately doubted the effectiveness of Interventions, especially against the context of an independent monetary policy and growing liquidity of financial markets. Furthermore, non-monetary causal factors undermined the monetary 'credibility' of the Fed; between 1988-1995 there were politically motivated swap lines extended to other economies, most notably Mexico when it underwent its own currency crises.

The Greenspan Fed had frequent discussions over U.S. policy on Interventions; by the end of 1989, many FOMC members felt continued cooperation with the Treasury over Intervention should come to an end. Sterilised Interventions came into collision with the Macroeconomic trilemma, where Policymakers cannot concomitantly sustain a fixed exchange rate, independent monetary policy, and capital mobility. Forex Interventions presented U.S. policymakers with more targets than independent instruments to satisfy them, breaking the Tinbergen principle of monetary policy; Greenspan himself said, *FOMC Transcript*, 3rd October 1989: "*we have too many policy objectives and only one policy lever*".

Following 1995, U.S. Forex Interventions occurred only on three other occasions, as of the author writing this chapter in 2012; against the Yen on 17th June 1998 and 18th March 2011, and against the Euro on 22nd September 2000. Shedding the "anachronism" of the past by 1995; Greenspan, *FOMC Transcript*, 28th March 1995: *"Much of our post Bretton Woods structure at the Federal Reserve is an anachronism"*.

Chapter 3

"Part of the weakness of the yen has been attributed to the rift between the Bank of Japan and the Ministry of Finance, beyond the more general political problem"

Forrestal

Figure 14: Monthly Japanese Forex Interventions in millions of Dollars against the U.S., 1973:03-2003:10, and Monthly nominal and real Yen/Dollar Indices. Additional Information: i) Yen appreciation registers a decrease in the Index, ii) Monthly Interventions are accumulation of Daily Interventions converted into nominal Dollars by the daily average Yen/Dollar spot rate, and iii) positive Interventions are purchases of Dollars.

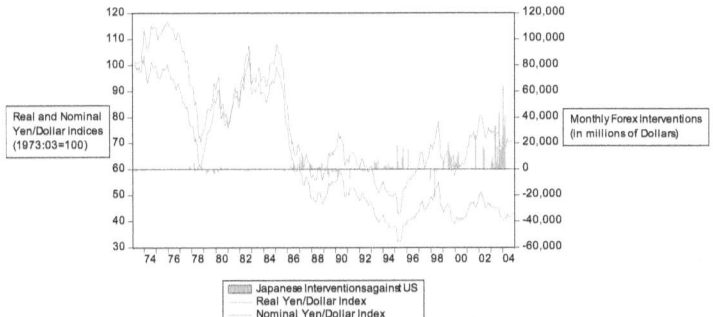

Figure 15: Monthly Japanese Forex Intervention in millions of Dollars against the U.S., 1973:03-2004:10, and % Valuation of the Yen against the Dollar. Similar to the methodology used in calculation of data for Figure 11 within the previous pages.

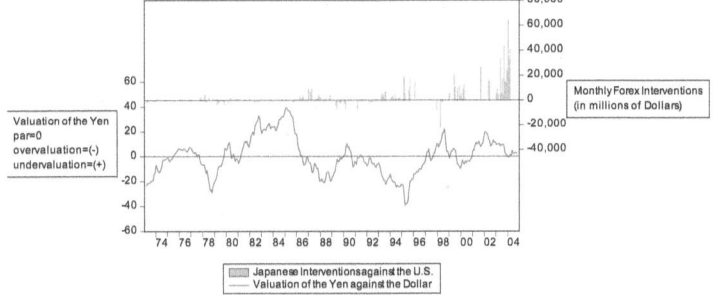

Figure 16: Daily Japanese Forex Interventions in millions of Dollars against the U.S., Daily Returns on Yen/Dollar, and Daily Volatility of Yen/Dollar, 01/04/1991-29/10/2004. Additional Information:i) Daily Interventions converted into nominal Dollars by the daily average Yen/Dollar spot rate, ii) Daily Returns are measured by % logarithmic difference of Daily Close Yen/Dollar rate between (t) and (t-1), and iii) Daily Volatilities are the squares of Daily Log Returns.

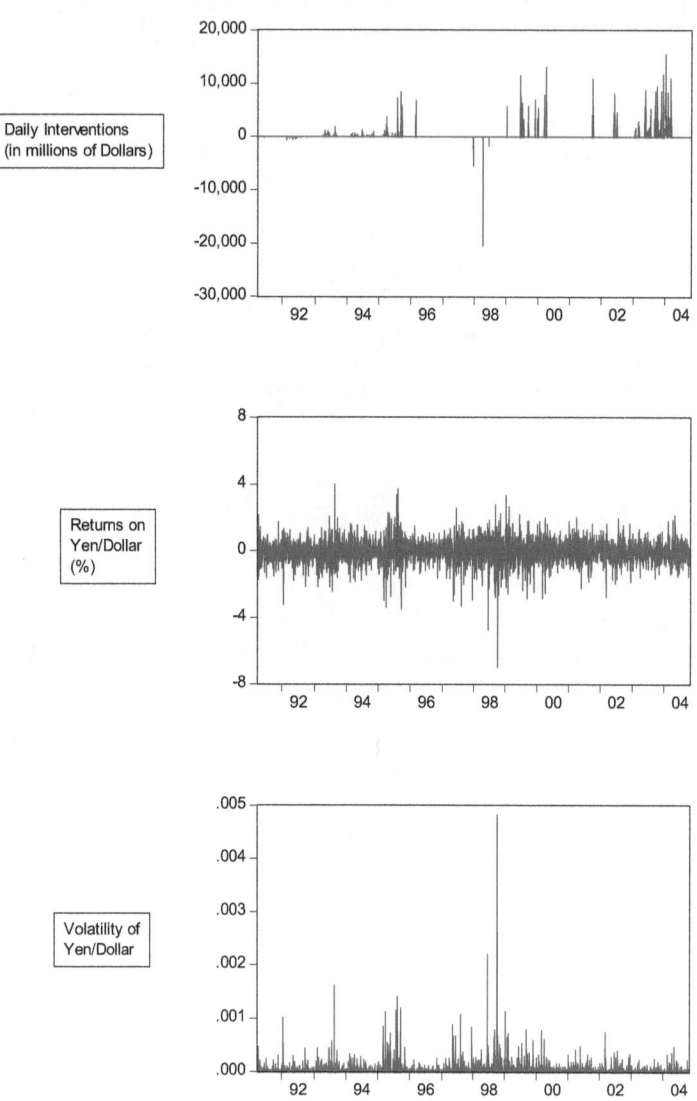

Japanese Intervention Regimes is institutionally similar to the Dichotomy between the Fed and the Treasury in U.S. Forex Interventions. However, the institutional supremacy of the Japanese Ministry of Finance over the Bank of Japan, its central bank and its agent in the Forex markets, is more pronounced than the U.S. Treasury over the Fed.

Japanese Intervention decisions belong typically to four individuals in the Japanese Ministry of Finance: Minister, Vice Minister for International Affairs, Director General of the International Bureau, and the Director of the Foreign Exchange and Money Market Division. Thus, allowing the Ministry of Finance to pursue Interventions without the cooperation of its central bank. For instance, the Ministry of Finance is able to automatically sterilise the Interventions, by being able to issue financing bills to the market to obtain Yen funds needed for Forex Interventions without the need for approval or compliance of the Bank of Japan.

Japanese policymakers have not revealed the data on Forex Interventions from 1973 to 1991 perhaps in light of their retrospective ineffectiveness; a thesis which is supported by the strong linear correspondence of the Yen in that period corresponding to Japanese Macroeconomic Development. Additionally, the Bank of Japan factored in Interventions in its monetary policy and thinking throughout Post-Bretton Woods.

Japanese policymakers in early Post-Bretton Woods pursued a 'leaning-against-the-wind' strategy countering short-term fluctuations of the Yen; supported by the analysis of Jurgensen, in *Report of the Working Group on Exchange Market Intervention.*

However, they also sought to counter medium-term and long-term Yen movements. Most early Interventions were against the Dollar due to a high proportion of Bilateral Japanese trade and financial transactions with the U.S. and Japanese concerns over the political reaction from a perceived overvaluation of the Yen/Dollar rate. However, U.S. policymakers, in particular the Fed in early Post-Bretton Woods, were reluctant to coordinate with the Japanese to stem the appreciation of the Yen; as notably recounted by the then Fed Chairman, William Miller, in *FOMC Transcript*, 21st March 1978:

"CHAIRMAN MILLER: The main one [problem], of course, is the yen. And I personally am not prepared to suggest that we get involved. The Japanese are extremely upset. It's a very serious political problem with the Japanese. I'd want to send high level people [there] to try to get some similar arrangements. I don't think that we really have the resources to deal with it. And I don't think the yen in international money markets represents the same kind of problem. I think the Administration is going to have to deal with the Japanese from a foreign policy point of view; I don't think we can really deal with it. As you know, their interventions are massive and even if there were some psychological basis for us having a $2 billion swap line with them, it could be used up so quickly. It wouldn't really make good sense; it doesn't seem so to me. But it's a very serious problem in terms of international relations; in terms of realities it's something else."

Through the encouragement of the U.S. Treasury, Ministry of Finance, and the Bank of Japan, the Yen depreciated in 1979. The depreciation overshot, leading to further Japanese counter-interventions to prevent domestic inflationary pressures.

Japanese concerns over a potential U.S. protectionist backlash led to a general acceptance of the Yen's undervaluation leading up to the Plaza Accords in 1985. Volcker and Gyohten record that the acceptance of Yen overvaluation was very much at the personal behest of Noboru Takeshita, the then Japanese Finance Minister, who was worried of a U.S. political backlash against Japanese trade. Japanese policymakers ambivalently supported an appreciation of the Yen/Dollar rate following Plaza; Japanese ambivalence characterised for instance by Figure 3 in Chapter 1, the author's changes in Dollar Reserve calculations indicate concerted counter-productive Japanese purchases of Dollars between 1986:04-1988:11 to counterbalance the depreciating Dollar.

There were additional concerns expressed by Japanese exporting industries of the damaging effects of an overshooting appreciation of the Yen following Plaza; Japanese labelled the rising Yen phenomenon as "Endaka", a state of the Yen which is oft-quoted since the late 1980s.

The institutional relationship between the Bank of Japan and the Ministry of Finance was further undermined following Plaza, as the former resisted attempts of the latter to dictate monetary policy to support the political coordinate of the post-Plaza U.S.-determined exchange rate policy. The Bank of Japan did not consult with the Ministry of Finance on a rate hike one month following Plaza; and likewise in 1986, the Bank of Japan did not comply with the Ministry of Finance's efforts to coordinate interest rates rises with the Bundesbank, and relative to the Fed. As an outcome of this lack of policy coordination between these Japanese Institutions, the following Act No. 89 of June 18, 1997 was legislated on revising the Bank of Japan Act from 1942; under Article 40, paragraph 3, of the 1997 revision:

"The Bank of Japan shall, when buying and selling foreign exchange on its own account or as an agent on behalf of foreign central banks, etc. or international institutions to cooperate with them as the central bank of Japan pursuant to paragraph 1, conduct the buying and selling for the purpose which the Minister of Finance specifies as constituting cooperation in the field of international finance, at the request, or upon the approval, of the Minister of Finance."

Indeed prior to 1997, the Ministry of Finance came under political and Japanese press fire in the 1990s for its role in coercing the Bank of Japan and trampling on its monetary independence in the 1980s. The attrition between the two Institutions led to a lessening of the effectiveness of Japanese Forex Interventions as recounted in exchanges in the *FOMC Transcript*, 27th March 1990:

"MR. FORRESTAL: I had another question, Mr. Chairman. Going back to the yen: Part of the weakness of the yen has been attributed to the rift between the Bank of Japan and the Ministry of Finance, beyond the more general political problem. But they did do the discount rate increase of 1 percentage point. Does that suggest that that rift has been healed or is that ongoing and will it prevent the Bank of Japan from taking further anti-inflationary steps?

MR. CROSS: It's hard to say. The rift went on for so long that by the time the 1 percentage point change was actually introduced it already had been totally discounted in the market and market rates didn't change. So, rather than being seen as a sign of forcefully getting hold of the situation, it perhaps was taken by a lot of people as still a following of events--following the curve or trying to catchup and being dragged along belatedly when circumstances forced it. So, it did not come out with a result that was strong and positive. Whether these differences are going to be less in the future is a little—

CHAIRMAN GREENSPAN: Actually, there is really a quite important difference between the Minister of Finance and the Governor of the Central Bank of Japan."

Following the bursting of the Japanese Asset Bubble the Yen drastically appreciated at the end of the 1980s, reversing some of the intentions of Louvre; Volcker and Gyohten considered the Plaza-Louvre process to be a "confused three-year process, the results of which were not very satisfactory". Despite a positive Uncovered Interest-rate Parity differential between Japan and the U.S., the Yen almost doubled its value against the Dollar between 1990 and 1995. Indeed during the early 1990s, there was an initial policy aversion by the Bank of Japan towards a Yen Depreciation fearing it would have an adverse upward effect on domestic prices and external balance; at its worst, this corroborates the wide information gap between policymakers and economic indicators during Post Bretton Woods.

The sudden Yen appreciation in the early 1990s was due in part of the Yen acting as a safe haven, as a consequence of the collapse of the cold war status quo ante and German Unification; the latter amplifying intra-European fragilities with the European Exchange Rate Mechanism; *Quarterly Economic Outlook*, Autumn 1992:

"More recently, however, the trend to buy yen has somewhat accelerated owing to heightened tension with respect to European currencies since the end of September and delayed economic recovery in the United States"

The appreciation also came from the rising use of a carry trade strategy against the Yen by private agents and fund managers on Global Forex Markets. The carry trade is a basic arbitrage strategy which undermines the Uncovered Interest-rate Parity condition: Investors invest capital in currencies with high nominal interest rates by obtaining it from currencies with low interest rates. Thus the currency of the former economies, with high nominal relative interest rate, appreciates.

The Yen appreciation, against the backdrop of a weakening Japanese economic outlook, led to further declines in Japanese exports and competitiveness. Additionally, there was a lack of enthusiasm amongst the other leading economies, including the U.S. and Germany, to continue Forex Interventions, let alone to coordinate further Interventions by the mid-1990s as recounted by Alan Greenspan following the 1990 G-7 Meeting in *FOMC Transcript*, 11th April 1990:

"[Japanese] asked several European central banks to act on their behalf using Bank of Japan funds to intervene against the dollar in favor of the yen in Europe. And I think there were one or two countries, including Switzerland, that did intervene on their own in dollars against the yen. The Swiss incidentally are endeavoring to move into the United Nations, assuming a referendum sgoes positively, but they also are seeking to obtain a 23rd seat on the [IMF] Board. It's up in the air at this stage. I think the French went in to be helpful. But the rest of us, as far as I remember, were there strictly only to the extent the Japanese had requested. We intervened in a very small amount."

The Japanese Ministry of Finance was unique in conducting large unilateral Forex Interventions so late in Post Bretton Woods. Between April 1991 and March 2004, Japanese Forex Interventions against the U.S. amounted to nearly $615 Billion. Whereas, Japanese Interventions against the Deutschmark/Euro were insignificant as were recounted in *FOMC Transcript*, 29th-30th June 1999. Nevertheless, the Japanese Interventionist Period under Post Bretton Woods is unique for its unparalleled demonstration in economic history towards directly aiming to control a country's exchange rates. During this latter period upto 2004, the individual median of Japanese interventions were $695 million, of which the median of dollar purchases was at least three times larger than the median of dollar sales reflecting Japanese concerns over Yen overvaluation prolonging their lost decade.

Ito and Yabu estimate an order probit model to show a negative 'leaning-against-the-wind' daily reaction by Japanese Policymakers to previous day's and/or last 21 days' Yen/Dollar movements over the period of 1991 and 2003. Negative 'leaning-against-the-wind' suggests a Yen appreciation the previous day or in the last 21 days tends to trigger a sale of the Yen.

Japanese Forex Interventions between 1995 and 2002 were more successful following the appointment of Eisuke Sakakibara at the Ministry of Finance's International Bureau; similar to the role played in the U.S. Interventionist Institutional regime by the Forex Desk at the New York Fed. Ito, in *'Is Foreign Exchange Intervention Effective?: The Japanese Experience in the 1990s'*, uses Sakakibara's tenure to identify a structural break in the efficacy of Japanese Interventions following 1995; similar to the findings of Fatum and Yamamoto, in *'Does Foreign Exchange Volume matter?'*, who use the Bai and Perron structural change test to identify 5th May 1995 as the structural breakpoint, just before Sakakibara's regime.

Reports in the press also suggested that the weak macroeconomic conditions within Japan by 1995 led to increasing public and academic calls for the Bank of Japan to intervene "almost without limit". Even U.S. Fed found the round of Japanese Interventions before 1995 to be "dubious", reiterated by Alan Greenspan in *FOMC Transcript*, 5th-6th July 1994:

"I would argue strongly about that because a goodly part of our official support is coming from the Japanese; they are in the market every day, just

picking up $100million, $200 million, $500 million, and I think the evidence that they are affecting the exchange rate is very dubious."

Following his tenure start, Sakakibara's credibility lent his comments great weight in the Forex Markets, compared to his predecessors: "Sakakibara said the dollar could fall to 103 [...]. Market Players drove the dollar down to 111", *The Nikkei Weekly*, Japan Economic Almanac 1998. During Sakakibara, Forex Interventions became infrequent but larger; the largest of which was a $20.4 Billion sale of Dollars on 10th April 1998. Interventions between 1995-2002 were more than 10 times larger compared to 1991-95. Sakakibara gained an almost sage-like Greenspan-esque status amongst private agents, markets, and the media, and was given the moniker "Mr. Yen". Under Sakakibara, the Bank of Japan Governor from 1998 to 2003, Masaru Hayami, wrote presciently in 1993 of a need for an "unexpected and perfectly timed" Intervention policy.

Also, during this period all Japanese purchases of Dollar led to same-day depreciation of the Yen. Helped by much media and public expectation in regards to a Japanese recovery when Sakakibara began his tenure; outlined most prominently in 'A Bold Campaign to end Endaka', 27th August 1995, by *Bloomberg Businessweek*.

However, Coordination with the U.S. had little effect on the probability of success of an intervention; nevertheless for the purposes of robustness there was a paucity of coordinated, compared to total, Japanese Forex Interventions. Only 22 of the 340 Japanese Forex Interventions between 1991 and 2004 were coordinated with the U.S due to the diminishing importance given of fulfilling Dollar exchange rate objectives at the Greenspan Fed.

Sakakibara term at the International Bureau was followed by Hiroshi Watanabe and Zenbee Mizoguchi; Sakakibara was appointed the Director General of the Ministry of Finance's International Bureau in July 1995, and became Vice Minister of Foreign Affairs in July 1997. Sakakibara retired in July 1999; however his immediate successor, Haruhiko Kuroda, carried on with Sakakibara's interventionist philosophy; which recently saw an uncanny revival under Kuroda's current term as the governor of the Bank of Japan.

During Watanabe and Mizoguchi tenures, Japanese Forex Interventions between 2003 and 2004 became frequent, Closed, less effective, and fell by half in size compared to Sakakibara's tenure. Ito shows Forex Intervention of One Trillion Yen led to 0.7% depreciation during 1995-2002 compared to only 0.38% in 2003-04. Furthermore, infrequent interventions depreciated the Yen by 2.1% and 0.45% during 1995-2002 and 2003-04, respectively. Ito defines Infrequent Interventions as those Forex Interventions which do not follow another Intervention in the preceding five business days. Japanese policymakers were concerned over the impact of deflation and export competitiveness on their economy which resulted in concerted unsterilised Forex Interventions between 1999-2003.

The costs of Japanese Forex Interventions during the 'lost decade' of the 1990s and early 2000s were small because of slow growth, zero interest rates, and deflation. Japanese Interventions were consistent and symptomatic of weak macroeconomic conditions; Early passages of the Monthly Economic Review, between 1991 until at least the 18th March 1994 edition, always began with *"Japan's economic growth remains weak without clear indication of imminent recovery"*.

Furthermore, in a liquidity trap the effects of unsterilised Interventions through changes in the monetary base do not influence interest rates and prices. However, some sterilisation would have been required if the Bank of Japan had an implicit bank reserve target. In fact, Ito estimates, due to the differential between the yields on Yen- and Dollar-denominated Financial Bills, the net interest incomes of Interventions for the Ministry of Finance between 1991 and 2004 totalled 5.4 trillion Yens due to net Dollar purchases. However, the Jurgensen report argued ex post profitability of Interventions in economic history bore little relation to ex ante Intervention objectives.

Table 4: List of Bank of Japan Governors, and corresponding Japanese Ministers of Finance and Prime Ministers, 1973-2004.

Bank of Japan Governors	Ministers of Finance	Prime Ministers
Tadashi Sasaki (December 1969-December 1974)	Kichi Aichi (December 1972-November 1973)	Kakuei Tanaka (July 1972-December 1974)
	Takeo Fukuda (November 1973-July 1974)	
	Masayoshi Ohira (July 1974-December 1976)	
Teiichiro Morinaga (December 1974-December 1979)	Masayoshi Ohira (July 1974-December 1976)	Takeo Miki (December 1974-December 1976)
	Hideo Bo (December 1976-November 1977)	Takeo Fukuda (December 1976-December 1978)

	Tatsuo Murayama (November 1977-December 1978) Ippei Kaneko (December 1978-November 1979) Noboru Takeshita (November 1979-July 1980)	Masayoshi Ohira (December 1978-June 1980)
Haruo Mayekawa (December 1979-December 1984)	Noboru Takeshita (November 1979-July 1980) Michio Watanabe (July 1980-November 1982) Noboru Takeshita (November 1982-July 1986)	Masayoshi Ohira (December 1978-June 1980) Zenko Suzuki (July 1980-November 1982) Yasuhiro Nakasone (November 1982-November 1987)
Satoshi Sumita (December 1984-December 1989)	Noboru Takeshita (November 1982-July 1986) Kiichi Miyazawa (July 1986-December 1988) Tatsuo Murayama (December 1988-August 1989) Ryutaro Hashimoto (August 1989-October 1991)	Yasuhiro Nakasone (November 1982-November 1987) Noboru Takeshita (November 1987-June 1989) Sosuke Uno (June 1989-August 1989) Toshiki Kaifu (August 1989-November 1991)
Yasushi Mieno (December 1989-December	Ryutaro Hashimoto (August 1989-October	Toshiki Kaifu (August 1989-November

1994)	1991)	1991)	
	Tsutomu Hata (November 1991-December 1992)	Kiichi Miyazawa (November 1991-August 1993)	
	Yoshiro Hayashi (December 1992-August 1993)	Morihiro Hosokawa (August 1993-April 1994)	
	Hirohisa Fujii (August 1993-June 1994)	Tsutomu Hata (April 1994-June 1994)	
	Masayoshi Takemura (June 1994-January 1996)	Tomiichi Murayama (June 1994-January 1996)	
Yasuo Matsushita (December 1994-March 1998)	Masayoshi Takemura (June 1994-January 1996)	Tomiichi Murayama (June 1994-January 1996)	
	Wataru Kubo (January 1996-November 1996)	Ryutaro Hashimoto (January 1996-July 1998)	
	Hiroshi Mitsuzuka (November 1996-January 1998)		
	Hikaru Matsunaga (January 1998-July 1998)		
Masaru Hayami (March 1998-March 2003)	Hikaru Matsunaga (January 1998-July 1998)	Ryutaro Hashimoto (January 1996-July 1998)	
	Kiichi Miyazawa (July 1998-April 2001)	Keizo Obuchi (July 1998-April 2000)	
	Masajuro Shiokawa (April 2001-September 2003)	Yoshiro Mori (April 2000-April 2001)	
		Junichiro Koizumi (April 2001-September	

		2006)
Toshihiko Fukui (**March 2003-March 2008**)	Masajuro Shiokawa (April 2001-September 2003) Sadakazu Tanigaki (September 2003-September 2006)	Junichiro Koizumi (April 2001-September 2006)

Chapter 4

"It has becomes increasingly difficult for the United States to fulfil its "natural" function of a key currency country"

Monthly Report of the Deutsche Bundesbank, November 1979

Figure 17: Monthly German Forex Interventions in millions of Dollars against the U.S., 1973:03-1995:12, and Monthly nominal and real Deutschmark/Dollar Indices. Additional Information: i) Deutschmark appreciation registers a decrease in the Indices, ii) Monthly Interventions are accumulation of Daily Interventions converted into nominal Dollars by the daily average Deutschmark/Dollar spot rate, and iii) positive Interventions are purchases of Dollars.

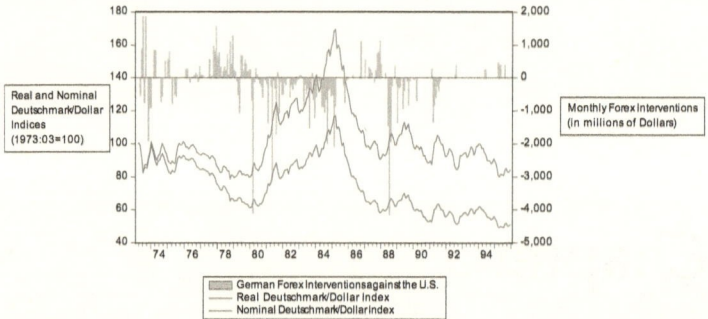

Figure 18: Monthly German Forex Intervention in millions of Dollars against the U.S., 1973:03-1995:12, and % Valuation of the Deutschmark against the Dollar. Additional Information: i) Monthly Interventions are accumulation of Daily Interventions, ii) positive Interventions are purchases of Dollars, and iii) Positive values indicate undervaluation of the Deutschmark.

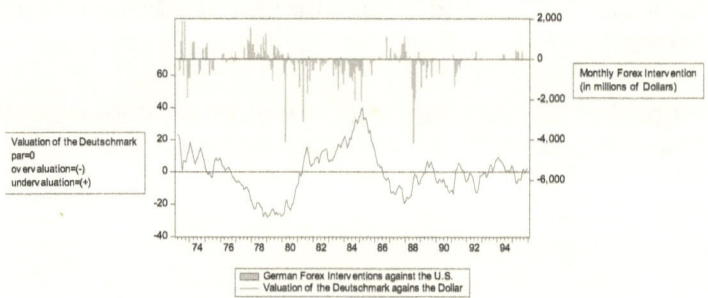

Figure 19: Daily German Forex Interventions in millions of Dollars against the U.S., Daily Returns on Deutschmark/Dollar, and Daily Volatility of Deutschmark/Dollar, 02/01/1976-29/12/1995. Additional Information: i) Daily Interventions converted into nominal Dollars by the daily average Deutschmark/Dollar spot rate, ii) Daily Returns are measured by % logarithmic difference of Daily Close Deutschmark/Dollar rate between (t) and (t-1), and iii) Daily Volatilities are the squares of Daily Log Returns.

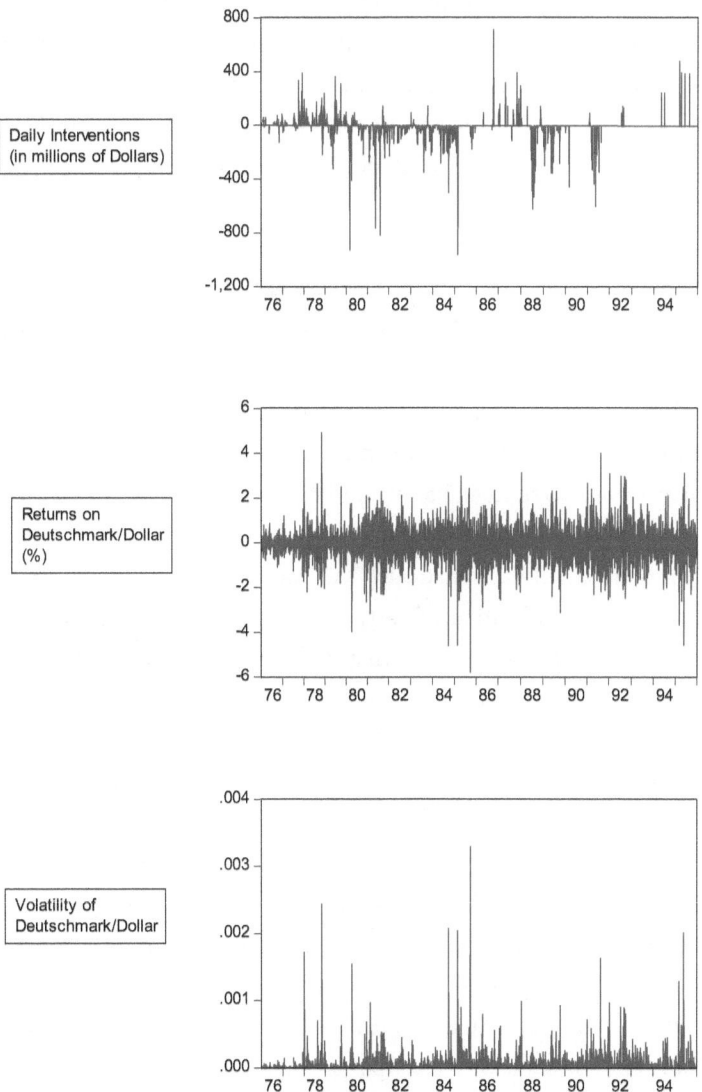

Under the German Forex Intervention Regime, the Bundesbank sought to conduct Forex Interventions with a similar philosophy to that of the Fed and Japanese Ministry of Finance. The Jurgensen Report accounted this in 1973 as *"[The Bundesbank] has sought from the onset of floating to counter disorderly market conditions, dampen erratic short-term exchange rate fluctuations and smooth out excessive swings in the DM/U.S. dollar rate over longer periods"*. The Bundesbank sometimes sacrificed its strong and credible anti-inflationary stance because of its exchange rate commitments.

German concerns over initial Deutschmark/Dollar overshooting led to Interventions in the late 1970s; The early Reports of the Deutsche Bundesbank themselves outlined the Bundesbank's Intervention policy was 'leaning-against-the-wind' in early Post Bretton Woods to mitigate exchange rate volatility and *"erratic exchange rate movements"*. Due to its implicit inflationary targets, the Bundesbank added more stringent conditions to swap lines for U.S. Interventions; the Bundesbank automatically sterilised its Interventions in the 1970s. Full Sterilisation of early Germany Forex Interventions was partly possible by the growing liquidity and expansion of the International Bond Markets following Bretton Woods Collapse.

The Bundesbank took its credibility from the 1957 law that required it to *"safeguard the value of the currency"*, which has meant it has aimed to keep annual inflation at or below two percent in Post Bretton Woods. Additionally there was the perception of conflict between the Bundesbank's commitment towards German monetary stability and increased Forex Interventions to prop up the, still nascent, European Monetary System by the 1980s; the European Monetary System was also partly supported through occasional coordinated French Interventions, most notably following Louvre the French intervened heavily to aid the rise of the Deutschmark but preserve the bandwidths of the whole European Monetary System.

From 1975 onwards the Bundesbank adhered to a monetary target; by 1987, the Bundesbank directly targeted the M3 supply; M3 consists of notes and coins in circulation plus domestic holdings of sight, time and savings deposits. The Bundesbank had growing concern in early Post Bretton Woods over the exact impact of Interventions on different measures of their money supply.

In August 1979, German Chancellor, Helmut Schmidt expressed concerns over *"American neglect and irresolution about the Dollar"*. This was also later recounted in the Monthly Report of the Deutsche Bundesbank, November 1979: *"It has becomes increasingly difficult for the United States to fulfil its "natural" function of a key currency country"*. Rising oil prices, with the Second Oil Crisis, led to larger German Interventions followed by higher interest rates. The impact of Forex Interventions on the German Monetary Base in order to support the weakening Deutschmark in 1979 led to inflationary concerns.

In general, whenever the objectives of exchange rates supplanted monetary targets the Bundesbank lost little market credibility in missing its M3 growth target as recounted and explained in the *Federal Reserve Bulletin*, October 1995:

"Whenever the monetary target has become less useful because of exchange-rate or other considerations, the Bundesbank has allowed M3 to miss its target temporarily and has suffered little loss of credibility. Another important factor has been the popular consensus against inflation, which is probably stronger in Germany than in most other countries"

Following the minimalist mindset of U.S. policymakers in spring 1981, German policymakers felt that their Interventions in the Dollar market had been adversely affected. In 1980-81, due to low relative interest rates, investor uncertainty over German economic policy, and other non-economic factors, the Deutschmark's value was supported by heavy German Interventions. The Monthly Reports of the Deutsche Bundesbank between 1980 and 1984, often wrote about the paradoxical and reverse trends of the Deutschmark with the ERM currencies and the Dollar, which raised complications in preserving the nascent European Monetary System.

The Bundesbank, under the presidency of Karl Otto Pöhl, feared a depreciating Deutschmark would bring inflationary pressures, threatening the Bundesbank's long held price credibility; reported in the *Monthly Report of the Deutsche Bundesbank*, February 1981:

"The nominal depreciation means first of all that German imports have become quite considerably more expensive; the mean increase in import prices is, in fact, much greater than the above-mentioned average rate because of the outstanding significance of the U.S. dollar as a currency for invoicing internationally traded raw materials and semi-finished goods. The depreciation of the Deutsche Mark thus not only aggravates domestic price and cost pressure but also places an additional burden on Germany's current account."

This price credibility anxiety often led to the Bundesbank unilaterally intervening in the Dollar markets against U.S. minimalist Intervention policy. Neumann, in 'Intervention in the Mark/Dollar Market: the Authorities' Reaction Function', estimates a simple reaction function for the Bundesbank which suggests the objective of

Interventions were to smooth changes in the bilateral real exchange rate.

Following the Plaza Accords, the Deutschmark strengthened against both the Dollar and the European Monetary System currencies; despite Inflation differentials favouring Germany which raised questions over the sustainability of the European Exchange system's parity rates. The Deutschmark appreciated drastically, following 1985, as it served as a safe-haven investment vehicle given market concerns over the direction and volatility of the Dollar: *"Recently, the Deutschmark has once again proved to be an antipole of the dollar"*, Monthly Report of the Deutsche Bundesbank, February 1987.

The Bundesbank worried that German Interventions against the U.S. would place further pressure on European Monetary System members to sell more dollars in order to concomitantly maintain their parities against the Deutschmark. As such as the European Monetary System became further embedded amongst the intra-European currencies, U.S. policymakers criticised the lack of German support for coordinated Dollar depreciation following Plaza. Similar criticisms were made following Louvre against Pöhl's staunch coordination-averse monetary policy. The Fed recognised that the Bundesbank's objectives under Pöhl were towards the maintenance of the European Monetary System, most prominently voiced in *FOMC Transcript*, 3rd November 1987:

"[German Policymakers] are more concerned about that than the Dollar exchange rate. They pretty much got all their trading partners pinned down in the EMS, and I think that's about all they care about."

Following Louvre, there was also a split between objectives between the Bundesbank and the German Finance Ministry; German Monetary policymakers in general were very reluctant for any declared policy coordination during Louvre. The Bundesbank overshot its real M3 targets between 1986 and 1988 as it resisted pressure to appreciate the Deutschmark. The Bundesbank was targeting an implicit range of 3-6% growth in M3 between 1986 and 1988, actual M3 growth rate was 8%, 8%, 6.7% for 1986, 1987, 1988, respectively.

Primary Sources suggest by early 1988, the Bundesbank was worried over the impact of an overvalued Deutschmark on its current account balance and trade. The Bundesbank's policy changed in reaction to the Deutschmark's movements over Plaza-Louvre: "exchange rates could not be stabilised through Interventions alone" as was recounted in the Monthly Report of the Deutsche Bundesbank, November 1988. By 1989, the Bundesbank announced an explicit M3 growth target of "about 5%"; more over this was in light of some six billion Deutschmark losses over Louvre through the Bundesbank's Interventions to support stabilisation of the Dollar. Bundesbank's Interventions had a deleterious effect on its balance sheets, and thereby monetary targets, leading the central bank to prescribe in its *Monthly Report of the Deutsche Bundesbank*, November 1988:

"The Bundesbank's foreign exchange and intervention policy must take due account not only of the exchange rate but also of the repercussions on monetary conditions in Germany. In the final analysis, it is a matter of stabilising price and exchange rate expectations (and thus in many cases interest rate expectations too), thereby promoting an economic upswing without tensions."

During German Reunification in 1990, the Deutschmark was politically determined at an exchange of one-to-one with the Ostmark, compared to the seven-to-one black market rate; this ensured an immediate 83% increase in the relative real wages of East German Workers preventing a mass economic migration westwards. Despite this, over the long-run the relationship between the Bundesbank's real M3 target and economic activity, interest rates, and net financial wealth following reunification remained unchanged; with the Bundesbank fervently using a high exchange rate to mitigate inflationary pressures. Furthermore, Reunification led to a high exchange-rate through a *"sustained boom in the west and a considerable need for resources in the east, the combined effect of which is a comparatively high interest rate"*, Monthly Report of the Deutsche Bundesbank, December 1990.

German Interventions during the 1992 European exchange-rate crisis amounted to more than 92 billion Deutschmark; *Monthly Report of the Deutsche Bundesbank,* October 1992: *"from the end of August to the end of September, the Bundesbank received foreign exchange totalling some DM 92 Billion as a result of support purchases of EMS currencies"*.

Most of these defensive interventions to protect the European Exchange Rate Mechanism were unsterilised due to the fears of higher interest rates. The 1992 Crisis was an extraordinary test of the character and determination of the Bundesbank, bringing to light the trade-offs between compromising its strict pursuit of domestic monetary credibility versus pan-European exchange rate stability; with a diminishing preference attachment given towards any Dollar Interventions following reunification regardless of the nature of the U.S. Interventionist regime.

The 1992 crisis sounded the death knell for German Interventions. Following the conclusion of European Monetary System, coordinated U.S. and German Interventions came to no avail against capital movement initiated by private agents. The Bundesbank was focused entirely on steering towards prudent fiscal and monetary German policy in its economic research; to the Bundesbank, by 1995, Interventions were no longer an instrument towards satisfying policy objectives, even in the short-term. German Monetary Policy became ever stricter at the initiative of the Bundesbank following the 1992 crisis; inherently, German policymakers believed that a *"monetary target is a clear stability signal [... with] the aim [...to] strengthen the inherent stability of the Deutsche Mark", Deutsche Bundesbank Monthly Report*, January 1995.

Along with U.S. Interventions coming to an end under Greenspan, by 1995 Hans Tietmeyer, the then Bundesbank President who shared a similar Interventionist philosophy with Greenspan, sought to bring German Interventions against the U.S. to a close in readiness of the monetary and exchange rate convergence towards a European Monetary Union by the Fin de Siècle, 2000. Greenspan himself best summarised this consensus on the outcome of interventionist philosophies shared with his German counterpart in *FOMC Transcript*, 15th November 1994:

"On the issue of intervention, we had some fairly interesting discussions earlier and I would like to lay some thoughts on the table that have certain implications for the future. I might add that, interestingly, my view about the way intervention works is something that Hans Tietmeyer and I happen to agree on...First of all, I think there is a view in the financial market place that intervention is far more effective than it actually can be. The analogy I like to use is that irrespective of what people in the markets believe, we can set the

federal funds rate wherever we wish to place it, and market trading, market activities of all sorts have no effect. There are people in the foreign exchange markets who believe that we as central bankers have the capability of doing the same thing to the exchange rate. A number of French financial officials clearly do believe that. A lot of commentators on the periphery believe that we central banks can fix rates where we choose.The truth of the matter that I think all of us have acutely recognized is that that "ain't the case."...We have all concluded that the only way we can have an effect in the exchange markets on a short-term basis--because nobody believes that sterilized intervention can have any long-term effect--is to catch the markets by surprise...There have been numerous occasions when we failed, when for one reason or another we either misjudged that the market didn't expect us to act or we felt that we had to act even though the market knew we were going to act in order to "show the flag" as the Treasury likes to say on occasion.I think the important point, however, is that we succeed some of the time because, if we create a presumption that we might intervene, we establish an atmosphere on the part of a lot of traders,who wish to take short overnight positions against the dollar, that they should be a little cautious. Indeed, it does seem to be the case"

Table 5: List of Bundesbank Presidents, and corresponding German Ministers of Finance and Chancellors, 1973-1999.

Bundesbank Presidents	**Ministers of Finance**	**Chancellors**
Karl Klasen	Helmut Schmidt	Willy Brandt
(January 1970-May 1977)	(June 1972-May 1974)	(October 1969-May 1974)
	Hans Apel	
	(May 1974-February 1978)	Helmut Schmidt
		(May 1974-October 1982)
Otmar Emminger	Hans Apel	Helmut Schmidt
(June 1977-December 1979)	(May 1974-February 1978)	(May 1974-October 1982)
	Hans Matthöfer	

93

	(February 1978-April 1982)	
Karl Otto Pöhl (**January 1980-July 1991**)	Hans Matthöfer (February 1978-April 1982)	Helmut Schmidt (May 1974-October 1982)
	Manfred Lahnstein (April 1978-October 1982)	Helmut Kohl (October 1982-October 1998)
	Gerhard Stoltenberg (October 1982-April 1989)	
	Theodor Waigel (April 1989-October 1998)	
Helmut Schlesinger (**August 1991-September 1993**)	Theodor Waigel (April 1989-October 1998)	Helmut Kohl (October 1982-October 1998)
Hans Tietmeyer (**October 1993-August 1999**)	Theodor Waigel (April 1989-October 1998)	Helmut Kohl (October 1982-October 1998)
	Oskar Lafontaine (October 1998-March 1999)	Gerhard Schröder (October 1998-October 2005)

Chapter 5

"My Impression of the years since I left government is [...the] frustration with what could be achieved, or simply change in the main personalities involved"

Volcker

Generally, Policy motives of Forex Intervention are to influence the value of the exchange rate; yet there are ex ante and ex post disputes within policy frameworks over the effectiveness, benefits, and costs of interventions. Many policymakers were ultimately concerned over the deviation of the exchange rate from its perceived fundamental value during the first half of Post Bretton Woods as repeatedly highlighted by Jurgensen in *Report of the Working Group on Exchange Market Intervention*.

Much of the policy discussions conducted within the differing Forex-Intervening Institutions of the G-3 Economies in Post Bretton Woods reflect at the lack of immediate success of Forex Interventions. Also, clear differences exist in G-3 Intervention policy at any one time; U.S. and German policymakers tended to intervene in order to strengthen their currencies in early Post Bretton Wood; whilst Japanese policymakers pursued the exact opposite strategy. However, G-3 Policymakers shared a common philosophy in the correction of the misalignment of exchange rates from the long-run equilibrium. Schwartz, in '*US Foreign Exchange Market Intervention since 1962*', mentioned "*it troubles [policymakers] that exchange rates (i) are transitionally volatile; (ii) exhibit medium-term variability; and that (iii) those not participating in coordinated intervention might be regarded as displaying a lapse of good citizenship in the world community*".

U.S. Forex Interventions in Post Bretton Woods have been debated in regular meetings of the FOMC; there has been a prominent evolution of U.S. interventionist philosophy due to the dominant but individually disparate Fed chairmanship of Burns, Volcker, and Greenspan, interacting with their corresponding administrations at the Treasury over Post Bretton Woods. The Fed expressed annoyance at the lack policy cooperation between itself and the U.S. Treasury. This dissonance of policy objectives was most observable following Plaza between Treasury Secretary, James Baker, and Volcker.

Following Volcker, Greenspan recognised the policy primacy over Interventions of the Treasury, initiating a different policy regime to Volcker. Even within the first six months of his chairmanship in the *FOMC Transcript*, 3rd November 1987, he declared:

"There have been significant disputes over the years as to precisely what the relationship is between the Treasury and the Federal Reserve with respect to the question of exchange rate intervention. As I understand it, even though there are disputable issues here, we largely tend to follow Treasury's lead in this question."

Volcker was critical of Greenspan's submissiveness: *"My Impression of the years since I left government is [...the] frustration with what could be achieved, or simply change in the main personalities involved"*, in Volcker and Gyohten, *Changing Fortunes, The World's Money and the Threat to American Leadership*.

Fed Chairmen have had differing responses to the U.S. political presidential administrations in place, causing delays in policy decisions, especially during an election year. Following the European Exchange-rate crisis in September 1992, policymakers recommended to *"wait until after [the November 1992 U.S. Presidential] election and until this [Republican] Treasury team or whatever Treasury team is prepared to talk about [further Interventions to arrest the Deutschmark's rise]"*, *FOMC Transcript*, 6th October 1992. Separately, *Bloomberg Businessweek*, in 'A Bold Campaign to end Endaka', 27th August 1995, reported that:

"Perhaps most critical has been a shift in Clinton Administration policy, which had favored a soft dollar...With the election looming, the White House wants a stronger dollar to drive down interest rates, boost the U.S. economy"

In terms of the dynamics of FOMC meetings, Greenspan, more so than other Post Bretton Woods Fed Chairmen, dominated policy discussions by corralling members towards a consensus; and at times Greenspan even persuaded members to move on without going into significant discussions of Intervention-related topics. Such domination at times led to FOMC meetings leaning towards "groupthink". Bell, in 'Ben Bernanke and the Zero Bound', argues the Greenspan Fed was dominated by "groupthink"—when individuals go along with what they perceive as the view of a group leader to maintain group harmony and avoid disapproval from others.

At times policymakers felt Closed Interventions were more effective compared to Open Interventions but this preference in particular during the Greenspan Fed saw philosophical resistance best outlined in the exchanges in *FOMC Transcript*, 5th-6th July 1989:

"MR. CROSS: ...we operated through a bank acting as an agent so that-- although the word does get around in some way and people who are following these markets closely can often tell a lot of what's going on--we did not go in openly buying foreign currencies. For the most part we had particular banks operating on our behalf in order not to show the extent to which the central banks were in there. We had gotten to a point where operating visibly was not really working very effectively and we thought it would be better to operate this way. Indeed, it has been much more successful. Remember, the other central banks have done the same thing, following our doing it. The Germans most recently, and the Japanese too, have been operating in a discreet manner.

MR. ANGELL: Do you think you were able to buy more cheaply by buying discreetly than if you had bought openly? Did you buy the portfolio--MR. CROSS: I think it was a lot more effective because we had reached a point where the market tended to feel that these rates were out of control--well, not out of control but beyond the ranges that the authorities wanted. And when they saw the central bank coming in there they almost took that as a basis [for believing] that the dollar was by definition undervalued. And they tended to hit it quickly. Now, in operating more discreetly we have been able to kind of encourage the dollar down without appearing to try to take on the market in a direct way...

MR. ANGELL: Well, Mr. Chairman I would make a comment: I just do not agree that it's appropriate for us to act in ways that are intended to confuse the markets or mislead the markets. I believe that markets work best when all participants have information as to what's going on. I am not a strong believer [in the view] that it made the difference because you did it in a discreet fashion lately. My guess would be that if you had operated discreetly during the previous period and you operated openly during this period you'd have found out that an open way would have worked in a better fashion. I just don't hold that these kinds of moves make that much difference. But even if they did, I do not believe it's appropriate for a government agency in a market society to be acting in such a manner. It's not appropriate for us; I believe it opens up the possibility for the charge of someone privately benefitting from what we do. So, Mr.Chairman, I would register not a dissent from the actions but an indication that if that were to continue I think I would have to object."

Despite Sam Cross, the Manager for Foreign Operations at the New York Fed's Desk, being an ardent supporter of Closed Interventions, over Post Bretton Woods, policymakers increasingly feared Open Interventions' success is undermined by counter-speculation conducted by private agents. Private expectations of an imminent Intervention only made it more ineffective.

Over Post Bretton Woods, the method of Forex Intervention changed as policymakers were backed up by substantial accumulated dollar and counterparty reserve holdings reducing the need for cooperative swap transactions; G-3 policymakers thought this lent them some credibility against private speculation as outlined in *FOMC Transcript*, 26th March 1991:

"The U.S. authorities combined--that is, the Federal Reserve and the ESF-- now hold marks with a market value of about $30 billion and yen with a market value of about $18 billion...on the positive side, looking at it from the perspective of where I sit, there certainly are some distinct advantages of our owning for the first time ever substantial currency reserves. Without having to belabor the obvious, not having to depend on the Bundesbank and other foreign central banks for all our financing at times of need gives us a great deal of independence as well as more of what I would call policyflexibility to deal with any exchange market flare-up, without necessarily having to change some of our policies at a time when that might not be wise or appropriate."

Also, the FOMC voiced Intervention concerns on occasions reflecting the lack of policy cohesion of the Fed with the Treasury over Interventions, as reiterated later on at the end of the Interventionist period in *FOMC Transcript*, 3rd October 2000: *"We can act as agent for the Treasury, but [...] we have an obligation not to intervene for the Federal Reserve account if in our judgment the Intervention is unwise"*. Similar policy conflicts existed between the Japanese Ministry of Finance and Bank of Japan. The Bank of Japan's Monetary Policy gave priority at times to the Ministry's exchange rate objectives however the Bank of Japan ultimately wanted to *"manage monetary policy with a view to securing price stability"*.

The Fed believed there was significant imperfect information within the Forex market which required frequent correctional adjustments to prevent the Dollar deviating from its perceived equilibrium value: *"The objective [of Forex Interventions] would be [...] to dissipate the present speculative fever [...], equilibrate underlying supply and demand relationship"*, FOMC Memorandum of Discussion, 9th July 1973.

At other times however members of the FOMC did not know the fundamental value of the Dollar: *"I don't know what a proper exchange rate is for the dollar. [...] I don't have a notion of what the proper exchange rate is from the standpoint of long-run equilibrium in trade and current account balances"*, FOMC Transcript, 17th January 1978. During the Volcker Fed, the exchange rate forecasting group met in secrecy reflecting the subject's taboo. Even the Jurgensen report concluded policymakers' assessment of the appropriateness of the exchange rate level relied on "eclectic, qualitative judgements". A sentiment reiterated also by the Bank of Japan Governor under the Sakakibara regime, Masaru Hayami, in 'Getting down to work on reducing the surplus', who said *"it is hard [for me] to determine exactly what rate accurately reflects the economic fundamentals"*.

Within FOMC meetings there were varied opinions expressed regarding the efficacy of Interventions and the fundamental value of the exchange rate most prominently expressed in the following exchange during *FOMC Transcript*, 28th-29th March 1983 :

"MR. ROBERTS: Why would we want to intervene? Do we know better than the market what the rate ought to be?

CHAIRMAN VOLCKER: At times.

MR. WALLICH: Yes.

MR. PARTEE: I doubt that.

MR. FORD: We like to think that, but I think we know[better]. Didn't you say you tried the arithmetic on this a lot of times and you could never figure out a formula for intervention?

CHAIRMAN VOLCKER: I could never figure out a formula for whether it should be 1 percent more or less in a day. I have no doubt at all in my own mind that the yen at 270, or wherever the heck it got to a few months ago, was too low and was greatly damaging to our interest and theirs. I have no hesitation at all in pronouncing that. I thought so at the time and I think so now."

By 1990s, many policymakers had concluded there "was no science" to Interventions, this was despite the Reagan administration having an unofficial target zone for the Dollar following Plaza. Additionally, on occasions FOMC members expressed their general ignorance over the fundamental value of the exchange rate, leading to a combination of counteracting sales and purchases of Dollars to provide 'stability'. Even the New York Desk did not have a long-term target in mind instead relying on a weekly rolling "sensible target" of the Dollar; neither was there an agreed-upon coordinated target zone amongst the G-3 economies.

The Treasury focused on containing volatility, "disorderly market", against a quarterly time horizon, "think about disorderly markets as a fifteen minute phenomenon; *FOMC Transcript*, 22nd August 1995:

"think about disorderly markets as a fifteen minute phenomenon [...] as a 24-hour phenomenon; or you can worry about whether there wasn't a bit of an *overshoot on a quarter-by-quarter basis. I think the Treasury's focus has been more on the quarter-by-quarter basis"*

More so, the statements during FOMC discussions of the Desk's Manager, Sam Cross, were expressed in retrospective defence of the Desk's actions and motives; on occasions, such as within *FOMC Transcript*, 26th March 1991, Cross maintained a vague position to defend the Desk's general operations especially when Cross was cross-questioned about the sufficient amount of reserves needed to maintain the supposed credibility of Interventions.

Cross' exchanges during this period reflected towards a captured interest within the institutional arrangement of U.S. policymaking on Interventions; Volcker and Gyohten, in *Changing Fortunes, The World's Money and the Threat to American Leadership*, observe the Institutional cross-nuances of U.S. Interventions not just between the Treasury and the Fed but also "the people in the New York Reserve Bank [...who] traditionally tend to be activists". However, such activism was weakened with Cross's error-prone successor—Bill McDonough. Later, Bill McDonough became vice-chairman to Greenspan.

By end of Greenspan's tenure, members of the FOMC recognised the growing sophistication of the Forex Market and Interventions running against "large positions" at the Fed based on "very sophisticated and very aggressive forms of program trading" by private agents; *FOMC Transcript*, 18th December 1990:

""[private financial institutions] now have at least one person [...] monitoring what is going on around the world. [...]; Corporations [...] are more involved than they used to be ,say, 10 or 15 years ago"

By the mid-1990s, the Desk used the difference between the implied volatilities of put and call options on Dollar rates to measure private agent speculation and the possible effectiveness of ongoing and imminent Interventions. This was in contrast to the Volcker Fed where there was a general admission of primitive non-economic and 'momentum' trading of early Forex Dealers in Post Bretton Woods.

During Greenspan Fed, many FOMC members felt the scale of Interventions would have to be proportional with the increasing volume of cross-border Dollar transactions leading to the size of Interventions having a negative effect on G-3 central banks' balance sheets, as Greenspan himself voiced in *FOMC Transcript*, 27th March 1990:

"One of the issues that we have to confront is that there is a globalization going on; there is no question that the amount of cross border transactions of every type is rising secularly against the nominal GNPs of the countries. And this is an irreversible process. So I think the issue is that were we to keep the proportion of intervention relative to the transactions constant, I would suspect that consumer and commercial banks are not going anywhere. But the ratio of our holdings relative to our total assets also would be rising secularly, and that's the problem."

The parallel balance sheet analysis of Interventions in the media also came to the same conclusion, expressed by policymakers, by the mid-1990s.

At the onset of the second Oil Crisis, in 1979, policymakers expressed a preference for a stronger currency under the International Monetarist view, of the belief of the underlying causal transmission mechanism from exchange-rate levels to inflationary impacts. Inconsistent Forex Interventions with lack of concomitant monetary and fiscal policy support further undermined the effectiveness of the former. *The Economist*, in 20th June 1987, deemed Forex Interventions not backed by policy changes as "not enough". Additionally, *The Economist*, 24th September 1988, recognised in pursuing exchange-rate stability, policymakers faced a conflict which arises between serving "two masters", those of the domestic and international economy. Some members of the Greenspan FOMC recognised quite early as well, following Louvre, the futility of influencing exchange rates without a strong commitment towards domestic and price stability. In supporting interventions to prevent the weakening new Euro on 22nd September 2000, immediate ex post FOMC discussions concluded at its ineffectiveness and cautioned against any future return to U.S. Interventions. Even in 2000, FOMC meetings hint at poor economic theory supporting Forex Interventions.

Additionally, profitability of Intervention was seldom in the original set of objectives for G-3 Central Bank Interventions; Sarno and Taylor, in Economics of Exchange Rates, measure profitability of Interventions as:

$$z_t = \sum_{k=1}^{t} \left[fx_k(s_t - s_k) + s_k(i_k^* - i_k) \sum_{j=1}^{k} fx_j \right]$$

Profits are the summation of two factors: i) the differential between end-of-period exchange rate at time t and the exchange rate at which foreign currency was purchased at time k, and ii) the interest differential between the two currency pairs at time k.

Many policy documents also indicate a story of G-3 policymakers' reluctance to commit and insufficient knowledge in hindsight of the motives of other central banks, during coordinated Forex

Interventions in regards to which, a lack of knowledge of the other players' motives and actions leads to an inferior outcome in the coordinated G-3 Intervention gameplay; *FOMC Transcript*, 3rd October 2000:

"Economists are agreed that sterilized intervention is unlikely to have any long-term effect. If there is a problem with policy fundamentals, then those fundamentals must be changed to achieve any lasting change in the value of a currency in the foreign exchange market. Based on extensive study and experience with exchange market intervention, economists have developed an overwhelming consensus that an exchange rate system should be either freely floating or thoroughly fixed through a currency union or a currency board. The halfway house of intervention is unstable and unsatisfactory. I know of no documented case in which an intervention episode from the beginning of a series of interventions to the end turned out well. I know of lots of cases that turned out badly. I've studied in considerable detail the intervention dynamic that began with the Plaza Agreement in September 1985 and lasted for several years. The conclusion from that analysis is that the Plaza intervention and its aftermath were costly for the United States and for Japan and the United Kingdom as well. Intervention during the 1980s and the early 1990s that attempted to maintain the European exchange rate mechanism did not work well."

At times, coordinated G-3 Interventions, as those following Plaza, were reneged if the terms of coordination were not made explicit and public from the beginning to allow G-3 public participants and private agents to judge retrospective mutual Intervention commitment compliance; concomitantly the precedent of written statement, or communiques, of International policy coordination conferences, starting with Plaza, were deliberately kept vague by some participants to prevent loss of credibility if reneged. Nevertheless, evidence shows G-3 Intervention Cooperation significantly improved over the course of Post Bretton Woods.

Policy regimes of Forex Interventions have come and gone. In order to make an impact on the level of the Yen in the later 1990s, at the Ministry of Finance Sakakibara favoured a philosophy of infrequent and surprise-laden larger intervention amounts in contrast to his predecessors; in Sakakibara, The day Japan and the world shuddered: establishment of cyber-capitalism, he said: *"The market was accustomed to interventions [before 1995], because they were too frequent [...and] had only short-term effects, [...] change in intervention philosophy and technique [was required]"*. Ultimately, infrequent Japanese interventions introduced an element of surprise for private participants.

Private agents interpreted any news development through the lens of the de facto Forex G-3 coordination regime of the period; such as, in August 1995 when the Bank of Japan attributed a subsequent depreciation of the Yen to the Ministry of Finance's public announcement of "Measures to Promote Overseas Investment". Another Instance was following Louvre, a press article, asserting that Treasury Secretary James Baker wanted to see the Dollar decline, led to an immediate depreciation only to be reversed following a meeting between German and U.S. policymakers in Frankfurt. Following Louvre, German policymakers were publically committed to coordinate monetary policy at the expense of domestic price concerns and in favour of maintaining an agreed upon coordinated G-3 exchange-rate trend; nevertheless, German public cooperation with U.S. Intervention policy post-Louvre did not occur.

In fact, G-3 Intervention coordinations were occasionally a façade for the institutional byplay occuring between the Fed and the Treasury; for instance, Treasury Secretary Nicholas Brady was instrumental in using coordination with the Bundesbank as a ruse to force the Fed's hand on easing monetary policy to support the Treasury's objectives in April 1991 leading upto the 1992 US Presidential Election Cycle. *The Economist*, 27th April 1991, went to press saying *"lower interest rates in Germany would virtually oblige the Federal Reserve to cut American rates, in order to brake the dollar's rise. Mr Brady does not, in fact, give a fig for global perspectives [...] he wants further cuts in American interest rates".*

Policymakers' economic understanding of Forex Interventions evolved over the course of Post-Bretton Woods; initially, there was little, if anything, said directly of the portfolio, expectations, and signalling mechanisms of sterilised Interventions. Early Post Bretton Woods, FOMC meetings implicitly mentioned the expectations mechanism of Forex Interventions, through influencing "market psychology". However, Early Post Bretton Woods FOMC discussions focussed more on the relative merits of contemporaneous public announcements of ongoing Forex Interventions.

The Desk's pattern for small scale and frequent interventions is best matched with the mindset of the portfolio balance mechanism. By the 1980s both the staff and the FOMC understood the distinction between sterilised and non-sterilised Interventions. Some believed Sterilised Interventions through the signalling channel were more effective when coordinated. The evolution of understanding led to "a sequence of policies" on Intervention over Post Bretton Woods.

Petering U.S. and German Interventions caught up with negative academic publications on the subject matter in the early 1990s, led most prominently by the monetarist school. The *FT Review of Business Books*, 28th September 1993, when reviewing this literature said: *"Leading monetarists have argued that the price of a foreign currency reflects demand and supply in the market. By definition it is the 'correct price'. Any attempt to subvert it ought to be doomed in the long run"*.

The Jurgensen Report, although falling short in accounting for the exact consequences of Forex Interventions, was a first in a series of publications on Forex Interventions which followed from the exchange rate modelling of Meese and Rogoff. In addition, the Fed completed ten studies in 1983 consisting of case studies, surveys, and econometric analyses on the subject. The Bundesbank also adopted similar views to Jurgensen in its reports thereafter, *Report of the Deutsche Bundesbank*, 1983: *"As in the past, the aim [of Intervening] was not to influence the basic trend in the dollar rate [...] rather, to react the one-sided orientation of the market and make market participants conscious of the growing exchange rate risks"*.

By 1989, FOMC members became sceptical of the signalling channel of Interventions in influencing private agents to support the Intervention action; *FOMC Transcript*, 3rd October 1989: *"we might engage in [Intervention] just for the sake of appearances on the grounds that the markets would then take over and that [Dollar overvaluation] would disappear. That hasn't happened"*.

Despite the eventual lack of confidence in intervening, the Fed continued to condone Interventions in the belief it would otherwise reduce their overall policy influence at the expense of the treasury, in the nexus of the U.S. Institutional framework; *FOMC Transcript*, 27th March 1990: *"The question that we have before us is not whether [Intervention] works in any substantial way [...], the question is whether or not we lose our ability to influence those [policy] decisions if we pull away [from Intervening]"*.

Furthermore, policymakers felt that the unintended consequences of the deterioration of global credibility of U.S. policymaking would outweigh in loss any monetary policy gains of severing the institutional Intervention relationship between the Fed and the Treasury. This, also, reflected on the growing changing perception by G-3 policymakers in the perceived tolerance of private agents of a global current account imbalance, most notable in financing ever larger U.S. trade deficits; *FOMC Transcript,* 27th March 1990: *"We also were concerned about the accumulation of assets, which ultimately would kill the value of the dollar. It turned out that the willingness on the part of the world to absorb claims against the United States [...] was much larger than anticipated".*

Chapter 6

"[Interventions are] exercise in futility"

Schwartz

In this Chapter, I provide a detailed evaluation on research and academic papers which have documented and modelled Forex Interventions in Post Bretton Woods by complementing the narrative of G-3 Interventions, given hitherto in previous chapters; additionally, I discuss the methodology and provide some models on Interventions.

Bordo, Humpage, and Schwartz catalogue Forex Interventions conducted during Post Bretton Woods in several working papers. In *'The Federal Reserve as an informed Foreign-Exchange Trader: 1973-1995'*, they evaluate the success of U.S. Forex Interventions using two specific criteria and a general amalgamated criterion. The two specific criteria are, firstly, if a Forex Intervention leads to the correct directional movement of the future exchange rate, and, secondly, if a Forex Intervention decelerates the incorrect directional movement of the future exchange rate. Both criteria are relative to present and past movements of the exchange rate within a pre-specified time window. The first criterion is a 'leaning-with-the-wind' policy, in that the Forex Intervention encourages a same direction exchange rate movement; the second criterion is a 'leaning-against-the-wind' policy which reverses an exchange rate trend. Their third criterion combines the two former criteria into an OR conditionality.

They find sixty percent of all U.S. Forex Interventions against the Deutschmark and Yen between 1973 and 1995 to be successful in fulfilling at least one of their criteria within an intra-day time window. However, the success percentage is similar to a random chance martingale process; suggesting Forex Interventions are a poor forecast of short-term exchange rate movements. This paper is an example of a typical event study approach to Forex Interventions in the literature. Generally, Event studies are used to assess the scale of the market's reaction to an event, how the event influences prices, and the structure and methodology of the effectiveness of a reaction to an event.

Bordo, Humpage, and Schwartz complement their results through probit analyses with the third criterion acting as the dependent variable and numerous other independent variables. In their probit analyses, the dependent variable (third criterion) takes the value of one when either Dollar movements are intervention consistent (first criterion) or trend Dollar movement is intervention consistent (second criterion), and zero otherwise. Independent variables include the size of U.S. Forex Intervention, whether the intervention was coordinated, whether an intervention occurred on the previous day, the number of days since the last intervention, the number of consecutive intervention days, and whether there was a compatible change in the federal funds or discount rate.

The probit analyses show the size of U.S. Forex Interventions consistently explains the likelihood of Intervention success. But they ultimately caution against a future return to Forex Intervention given the absence of sufficient knowledge by policymakers of private information in the Forex markets.

Due to infrequent Forex Interventions as a proportion of the aggregate number of business weekdays in Post Bretton Woods, probit and logit analyses are frequently used in the Intervention literature; Such that Intervention takes a respective value of 1 or 0 if

$|Int|_t > 0, Int_t = 0$

$Int_t = \beta X_t' + \varepsilon_t$

Where ε_t is either a normal or logistic distribution for Probit and Logit analyses, respectively. In both cases the regressors determines the conditional probability such that for distribution functions of the standard normal and logistic are reflected as following, respectively:

$\pi_t = \Phi(\beta X_t')$ and $\pi_t = \Lambda(\beta X_t')$

Small amount of intervention predictions leads to incorrect forecast errors. Baillie and Osterberg, and Dominguez first proposed the probit analyses with a binary choice dependent variable of Forex Intervention. Fratzscher uses a Logit model for measuring the impacts of publically announced statements on Forex-related policy and Interventions relative to past exchange rate movements. Fratzscher finds Interventions are more frequent when the deviation of the domestic currency from its average Purchasing Power Parity level is larger and exchange rate volatility is higher. Neely also shows that U.S. policymakers tend to purchase Dollars when the Dollar is undervalued compared to a Purchasing Power Parity-based fundamental value, and sell Dollars otherwise.

Fatum and Hutchison estimate an Intervention Reaction function from which they derive a 'propensity score' to calculate the counterfactual exchange rate movement; through which they demonstrate the effectiveness of sporadic and infrequent Japanese Interventions. However, Reaction functions are subject to the 'Lucas Critique'. In that evaluating alternative policy using reduced-form econometric specifications would produce misleading results because expectations and behaviour would differ over time leading to variations in policy.

Over Post Bretton Woods, changes in the economic environment from stagflation to full-fledged monetary independence of central banks would lead to unstable structural parameters as central bank Intervention Functions would be concomitantly unstable. To address these structural changes, Bordo, Humpage, and Schwartz subdivide their periods to check for structural breaks and robustness of their Intervention Criteria.

There is some ambiguity as to the effectiveness of Closed Forex Interventions. Bordo, Humpage, and Schwartz find Closed Interventions empirically explain little of the probability of the success of an intervention; whilst, Bhattacharya and Weller, and Vitale use theoretical models to demonstrate the potential effectiveness of a Closed Intervention. Additionally, the Jurgensen report found sterilised Interventions were less effective than unsterilised, and Interventions in conjunction with fiscal and monetary policy changes had a larger impact.

Event study approaches within the Forex literature attempt to overcome the simultaneity bias of the endogeneity between Interventions and exchange rates. Generally, within an event study the behaviour of the exchange rate ex ante to the Intervention is compared with the exchange rate ex post; papers vary in their time windows from one to thirty days. Event study approaches have an advantage over time series analyses in that they are not restricted to assess the effectiveness of Interventions according to an estimated coefficient. Different measures of success criteria in an event study approach include smoothing or reversing an exchange rate trend, assuaging exchange rate volatility, or influencing the direction of the exchange rate level. Fatum and Hutchison use non-parametric sign and match sample test to verify the relationship between Interventions and success criteria. Event studies can lead to biased results if they do not incorporate other important components which contain explanatory content for exchange rate movements. Additionally, the approach requires an a priori knowledge of the underlying Intervention motive of policymakers.

Examples of event study approaches include Fatum and Hutchison for Japanese Forex Interventions between 1991 and 2000, who conclude the effectiveness of the intervention is positively dependent on the size and coordination regardless of whether the intervention was Closed or if it was associated with compatible parallel monetary policy change; additionally, Fatum and Hutchison find in another paper there is no reliable relationship between Interventions and Federal Funds Futures, in that U.S. Interventions did not signal future monetary policy regimes. Humpage and Osterberg compare

U.S. Interventions to the same-day exchange rate movement between 1985 and 2007, concluding sterilised Interventions cannot regularly influence exchange rate movements because of the lack of an informational edge by central banks over private agents.

For time-series analyses, Lewis discovers over weekly horizons Forex Interventions granger causes future U.S. monetary policy variables; suggesting the signalling mechanism is at work. In contrast, Humpage conducts a time series analysis of U.S. Forex Interventions over 1984-1987; the null hypothesis rejects the operation of the signalling mechanism; the Null Hypothesis of $\beta_1 = 1, \beta_{2i} > 0$ Is rejected in: $$s_t = \beta_0 + \beta_1 s_{t-2} + \sum_{i=1}^{p} \beta_{2i} INT_{t-i} + \sum_{j=1}^{q} \beta_{3j}(i_{t-j} - i^*_{t-j}) + \varepsilon_t$$

Where the three explanatory components are twice-lagged nominal exchange rate; in turn, which are a proxy for the expected exchange rate, Interventions, and Interest rate differentials.

Humpage and Osterberg find similar results controlling for GARCH in the error term; whilst, Dominguez estimates different effects of Intervention for the same sample period.

Survey evidence, in particular, by Cheung and Chinn supports the asymmetric information mechanism. Popper and Montgomery argue central banks aggregate private information of individual traders, revealing this information through Forex Interventions. Furthermore, if private agents base their strategies on their guesses of how others would behave then a self- fulfilling outcome would result; Ito calls this a sunspot in the sunspot equilibrium.

Dominguez discusses how private agents, through the order-flow framework, trader heterogeneity, and information asymmetry, magnify the actual impact of Forex Interventions. Bordo, Humpage, and Schwartz also use their three criteria to test for the efficacy of the expectations mechanism. The criteria are based on the assumption that interventions are successful if they convey relevant private information about exchange rates to markets. Nevertheless, it is difficult to link short-run movements in exchange rates to fundamentals. Shleifer and Vishny show traders are constrained by risk aversion and principal-agent problems; whilst Klein and Lewis explore how learning and information problems can affect exchange rates.

Chaboud and Humpage test for the effectiveness of Japanese Forex Interventions between 1991 and 2004 using probit analyses. Chaboud and Humpage, also, carry out an events study using four success criteria of Forex Interventions similar to those used in Bordo, Humpage, and Schwartz. In general, they argue large central bank interventions should result in temporary adjustments of exchange rates and coordinated interventions with the U.S. have some explanatory power for successful interventions. The Jurgensen report states coordinated Interventions with other central banks signals to private agents a commitment towards a collective and credible policy on exchange rates.

Ito tests for the effectiveness of Japanese Forex Interventions, in multiple papers, using the following baseline specification:

$\Delta s_t = \beta_0 + \beta_1 \Delta s_{t-1} + \beta_2 (s_{t-1} - s_{t-1}^{MA}) + \beta_3 Int_t + \beta_4 IntUS_t + \beta_5 IntIN_t + \varepsilon_t$

Δs_t is the change in the Yen/Dollar rate, s^{MA} is the 180 days moving average of the rate, Int_t is Japanese Forex Intervention, $IntUS_t$ is coordinated U.S.-Japanese Forex Intervention, and $IntIN_t$ is Forex Intervention which does not follow another Intervention in the preceding five business days.

Ito demonstrates coordinated Interventions, and certain policy regimes lead to successful Forex Interventions. Also, Ito and Yabu use an ordered probit model to estimate policymakers' reaction function to show Japanese Forex interventions are 'leaning-against-the-wind'.
There is little consensus in the Forex literature on the impact of Interventions on exchange rate volatility; Schwartz, in *'US Foreign Exchange Market Intervention since 1962'*, famously concluded Forex Interventions as an "exercise in futility" which is likely to increase uncertainty and volatility. Dominguez finds Interventions increase volatility over short time horizons. Beine et al. do not observe a permanent effect of a coordinated intervention on the realised volatility of the Deutschmark/Dollar rates. Frankel et al. discover Japanese Forex Interventions increases the volatility of the Yen. Hashimoto and Ito use high- frequency data over short time windows, of thirty minutes or less, to demonstrate the significant and immediate reactions of Dollar/Yen rates and realised volatility to macroeconomic news announcements. Fatum and Yamamoto examine the impact of the size of Intervention volume on exchange rate using a twenty-year time series, finding that Intervention volume linearly affects the exchange rate.

Sarno and Taylor, and Neely give comprehensive theoretical and methodological coverages of the literature on Forex Interventions; Sarno and Taylor find increasing integration of capital market have reduced the effectiveness of the portfolio channel and both report mixed evidence on the effectiveness of Interventions. Furthermore,

Neely surveys central bank reactions to Interventions and finds policymakers remain convinced that Interventions are effective in changing the exchange rate. Neely, in another study, reports 17 of the 22 central bankers surveyed 'agree or strongly agree' that larger Interventions increase the probability of a successful Intervention.

For modelling exchange rates Interventions are seldom mentioned. In their seminal paper, *'Empirical Exchange Rate Models of the Seventies: Do they fit out of sample?'*, Meese and Rogoff found standard models of exchange rate determination failed to outperform a random walk. Early academic work focused on an asset approach to exchange rate determination pioneered by Dornbusch, Frenkel, Mussa, inter alia; the approach theoretically explained exchange rate volatility not only on the demand and supply of imports and exports but also on the expectations of the future level of output and money supplies.

Additionally, Flood and Rose show macro-fundamentals are poor predictors of exchange rate movements. Engel et al., and Engel and West argue exchange rates may not be distinguishable from a random walk because currency movements occur due to changes in expectations about future fundamentals. Obstfeld explains the movements in Japanese real exchange rates through relative real sectoral productivity growth using the Harrod-Balassa-Samuelson framework.

Kim uses a SVAR to overcome the simultaneity problems of Interventions and exchange rate movements by demonstrating the impulse responses of Forex shocks on exchange rate fluctuations are larger than monetary policy shocks. Kim used identifying restrictions that allowed exchange rate to impact Interventions and monetary policies' influence on the exchange rate. The results from Kim suggest U.S. Interventions were effective over the period 1973-1996. An and Sun replicate Kim's SVAR for Japanese Forex Interventions between 1991 and 2004, they find Forex Interventions are not effective and there is no conclusive evidence between the concrete linkages between Monetary policy, Interventions, and exchange rate dynamics. Kalyvitis and Skotida show the effects of U.S. monetary policy shocks on the delayed overshooting of the Sterling, Deutschmark and Yen, and their respective subsequent Forex Interventions. Ozcelebi and Yildirim construct a SVAR to explore the relative nominal, real and output dynamics between Germany, Russia, and Turkey.

In summary, there is little, if any, unanimity among Intervention studies on the size and effect of Intervention on the level and trend of exchange rates. Papers vary by time periods, data sources, and estimation methodology. Studies including Louvre and Plaza find Interventions have a significant effect on exchange rates. Whereas, those studies attempting to control for simultaneity are less likely to find a significant effect.

Chapter 7

"One problem in assessing whether interventions have delivered the intended goal is that the objectives followed by the central banks are rarely known"

Beine at al.

Measuring the impact of Forex Interventions is mired in problems of the exact intention of policymakers and endogeneity. Beine at al., in *'The Impact of FX Central Bank Intervention in a Noise Trading Framework'*, said: *"One problem in assessing whether interventions have delivered the intended goal is that the objectives followed by the central banks are rarely known [...], the objectives are likely to change over time"*.

The limitation on availability of Intervention data only goes to compound the problem; of those Interventions which are published, intra-day information is absent negating the robustness of short-term studies. Furthermore, Interventions quickly react to exchange rate movements and trend, and other variables, leading to exchange rates and Interventions to be determined simultaneously in the short-run.

Decisions to intervene can be threefold; either it is endogenous to prior exchange rate movements, or policymakers intervene with the intention of influencing future movements alone, or both. Additionally, measuring the causal impact of Interventions on exchange rates is undermined by simultaneity bias. The bias exists for instance when, suppose, policymakers react through: $Int_t = \beta \Delta s_t + v_t$ and the impact of Intervention is measured by $\Delta s_t = \alpha Int_t + \varepsilon_t$; the reduced form equates $Int_t = \frac{1}{1-\alpha\beta} v_t + \frac{\beta}{1-\alpha\beta} \varepsilon_t$ with $Cov(Int_t, \varepsilon_t) \neq 0$. Thus OLS estimator for the impact of Interventions on exchange rate is biased such that $\hat{\alpha} = \alpha + \frac{1}{\sum_{t=1}^{n} Int_t^2} (Cov(Int_t, \varepsilon_t))$; with similar reasoning, β too is biased.

Using one-period lagged exogenous component somewhat solves simultaneity; however this method would misrepresent the true effect of Intervention on private agent expectations because part of this effect may already be captured in the lagged values of the dependent variable.

Another method would be to take intra-daily open and close exchange rate data. However, this assumes daily Intervention is conducted during business hours between those points; this assumption is supported by Dominguez. Dominguez, 'The Market Microstructure of Central Bank Intervention', analyses Reuters reports of G-3 Interventions from 1989-1993. Dominguez indicates central banks intervene during business hours in their respective markets. Adler and Tovar estimate the effect of Forex Interventions through panel specification which accounts for heterogeneous reaction function of central banks. Additionally, they focus on short-term time-series from periods of significant global shocks which reduces omitted variable bias from unobservable country- specific shocks.

Using other estimations such as Instrumental Variables would produce biased estimators and hypothesis tests with weak instruments. Also, it is difficult to estimate the counterfactual of the exchange rate and other components in the absence of an Intervention; Ito measures Forex Intervention success against two counterfactuals, that of a random walk and linear trend. Ito applies the following restriction if the exchange rate movement follows a random walk:

$\beta_0 = \beta_1 = \beta_2 = 0$

In:

$$\Delta s_t = \beta_0 + \beta_1 \Delta s_{t-1} + \beta_2 (s_{t-1} - s_{t-1}^{MA}) + \beta_3 Int_t + \beta_4 IntUS_t + \beta_5 IntIN_t + \varepsilon_t$$

With all of the above accounts in mind, I model the impact of G-3 Forex Interventions on exchange rate determination through SVAR. Firstly, however, I graphically conduct event studies based on the responsiveness of Interventions to Fundamental levels of the exchange rate and the effects of Intervention regimes on Monthly Forward and Spot rates. Policymakers' exact specification for their fundamental exchange rate is not specified. However, using a regression of a quadratic time-trend and relative price levels I estimated the long-run Fundamental levels. The quadratic time trend, which is highly statistically significant for all estimations, permits a time varying Balassa-Samuelson effect. In figure 20, the percentage Logarithmic Difference between the red and blue lines is the over- or under- valuation of the exchange rate.

Figure 20: Long-run Fundamental Deutschmark/Dollar Level.

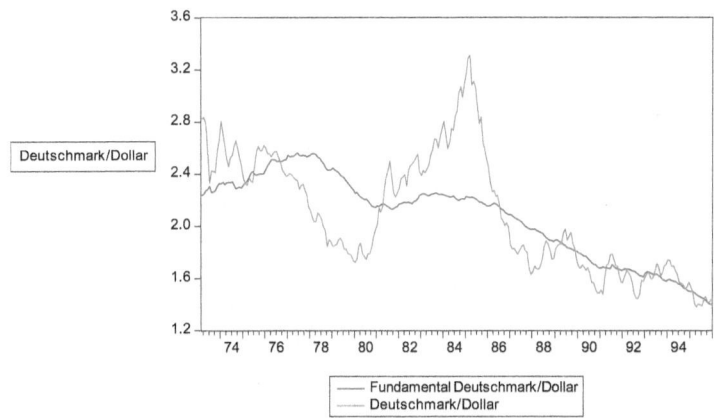

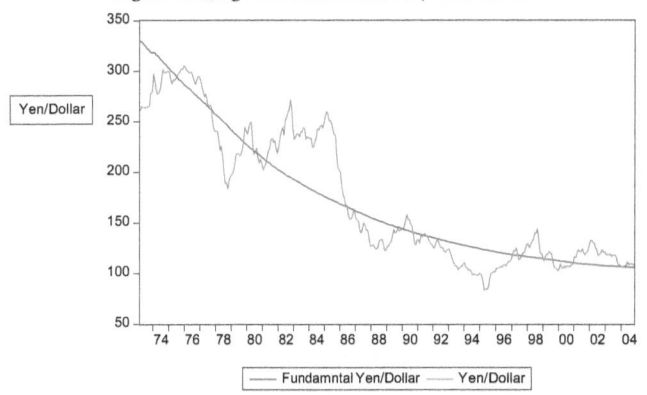

Figure 21: Long-run Fundamental Yen/Dollar Level.

91

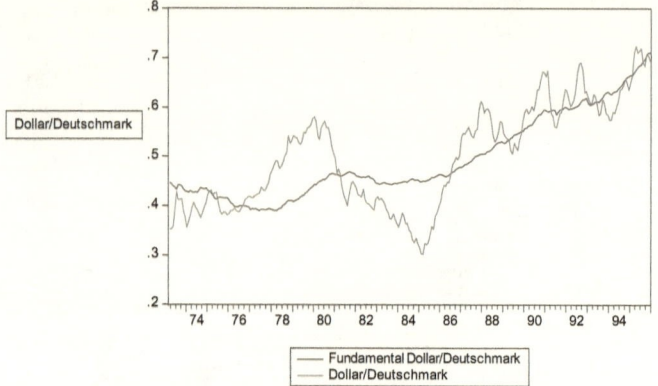

Figure 22: Long-run Fundamental Dollar/Deutschmark Level.

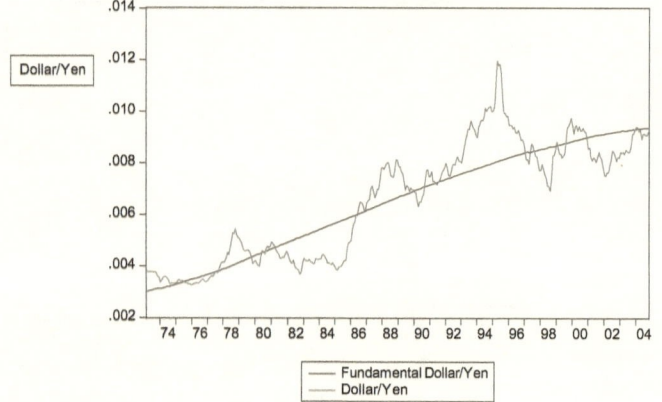

Figure 23: Long-run Fundamental Dollar/Yen Level

A preliminary hypothesis would suggest for the first study, policymakers are responsive to the fundamental valuation of their currencies and their corresponding reaction function would suggest compatible changes in ex ante and ex post valuations to a Forex Intervention. For Instance, a positive U.S. Intervention at time t—consisting of purchases of Dollars—may reduce the changes in increasing undervaluation of the Dollar against the Deutschmark or the Yen between (t-(t-1)) and ((t+1)-t) or reverse the changes from positive to negative; the former is indicative of 'leaning-against-the-wind' and the latter is 'leaning-with-the-wind'. Taking this into account the following second study measures the effectiveness of an Intervention through compatible monthly changes in real and nominal 3-month forward and spot rates. For Instance, a positive U.S. Intervention at time t should lead to a positive change in the spot and forward Deutschmark/Dollar or Yen/Dollar rate between (t+1)-t; where t is measured in months.

Figure 24: Scatterplot with red regression line of Nonzero Bilateral Monthly G-3 Forex Interventions in Post Bretton Woods, 1973:03-2004:10, in millions of Dollars measured at time t, against the respective % changes between (t)-(t-1), the % level at (t), and % changes between (t+1)-(t), in the Valuation of the Dollar against the Deutschmark and Yen. Additional Information: i) positive Interventions are purchases of Dollars, and ii) Positive values indicate undervaluation of the Dollar against the Deutschmark and Yen at time t.

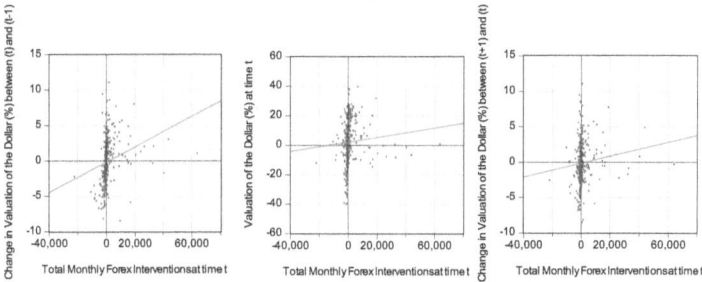

Figure 25: Scatterplot with red regression line of Nonzero Monthly U.S. Forex Interventions in Post Bretton Woods against Germany and Japan, 1973:03-1995:12, in millions of Dollars measured at time t, against the respective % changes between (t)-(t-1), the % level at (t), and % changes between (t+1)-(t), in the Valuation of the Dollar against the Deutschmark and Yen.

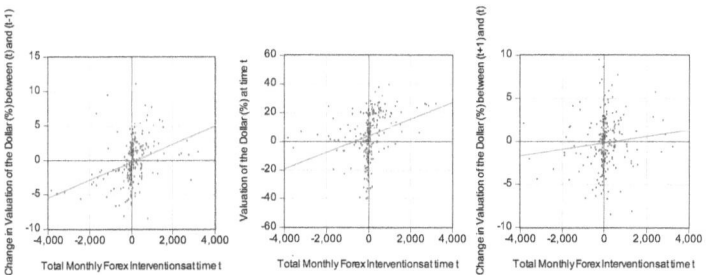

Figure 26: Scatterplot with red regression line of Nonzero Monthly U.S. Forex Interventions against Germany and Japan under the Burns and Miller Fed, 1973:03-1979:07, in millions of Dollars measured at time t, against the respective % changes

between (t)-(t-1), the % level at (t), and % changes between (t+1)-(t), in the Valuation of the Dollar against the Deutschmark and Yen.

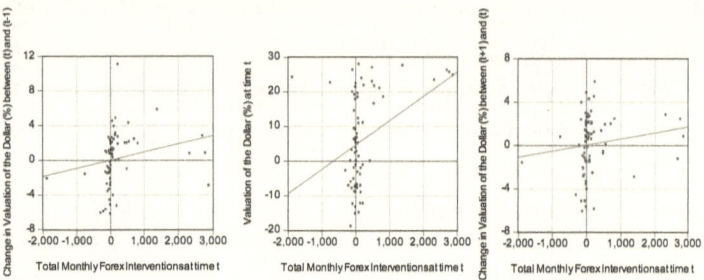

Figure 27: Scatterplot with red regression line of Nonzero Monthly U.S. Forex Interventions against Germany and Japan under the Volcker Fed, 1979:08-1987:07, in millions of Dollars measured at time t, against the respective % changes between (t)-(t-1), the % level at (t), and % changes between (t+1)-(t), in the Valuation of the Dollar against the Deutschmark and Yen.

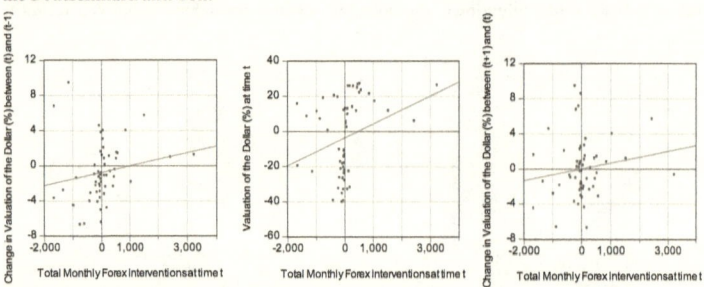

Figure 28: Scatterplot with red regression line of Nonzero Monthly U.S. Forex Interventions against Germany and Japan under the Greenspan Fed, 1987:08-1995:12, in millions of Dollars measured at time t, against the respective % changes between (t)-(t-1), the % level at (t), and % changes between (t+1)-(t), in the Valuation of the Dollar against the Deutschmark and Yen.

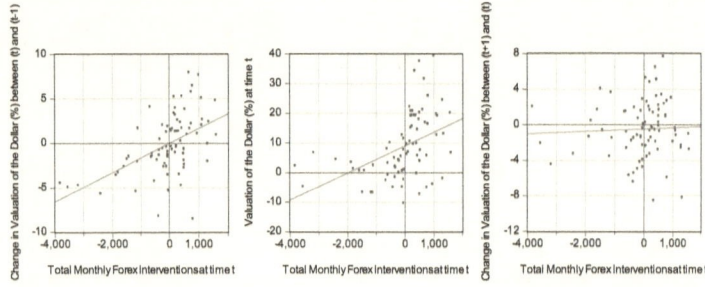

Figure 29: Scatterplot with red regression line of Nonzero Monthly Japanese Forex Interventions against the U.S., 1973:03-2004:10, in millions of Dollars measured at time t,

against the respective % changes between (t)-(t-1) , the % level at (t) , and % changes between (t+1)-(t) , in the Valuation of the Yen against the Dollar.

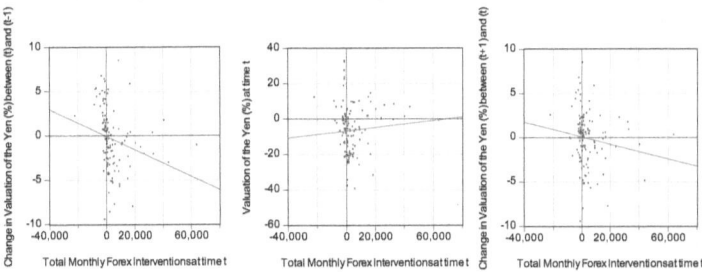

Figure 30: Scatterplot with red regression line of Nonzero Monthly Japanese Forex Interventions against the U.S. under the Japanese Interventionist Period, 1991:04-2004:10, in millions of Dollars measured at time t, against the respective % changes between (t)-(t-1), the % level at (t), and % changes between (t+1)-(t) , in the Valuation of the Yen against the Dollar.

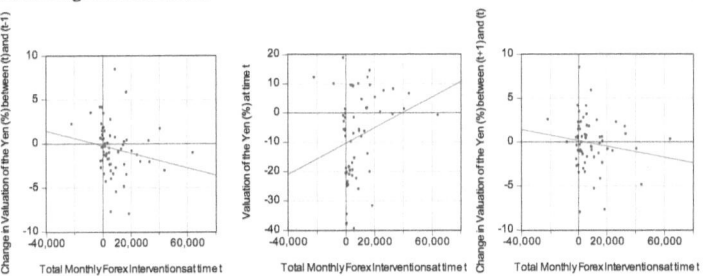

Figure 31: Scatterplot with red regression line of Nonzero Monthly Japanese Forex Interventions against the U.S. under Sakakibara, 1995:07-1999:07, in millions of Dollars measured at time t, against the respective % changes between (t)-(t-1), the % level at (t), and % changes between (t+1)-(t), in the Valuation of the Yen against the Dollar.

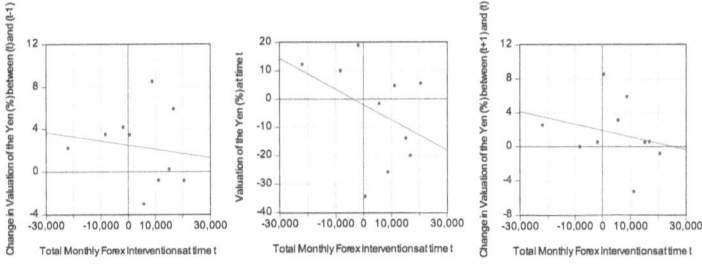

Figure 32: Scatterplot with red regression line of Nonzero Monthly German Forex Interventions against the U.S., 1973:03-1995:12, in millions of Dollars measured at time t, against the respective % changes between (t)-(t-1) , the % level at (t) , and % changes

between (t+1)-(t) , in the Valuation of the Deutschmark against the Dollar.

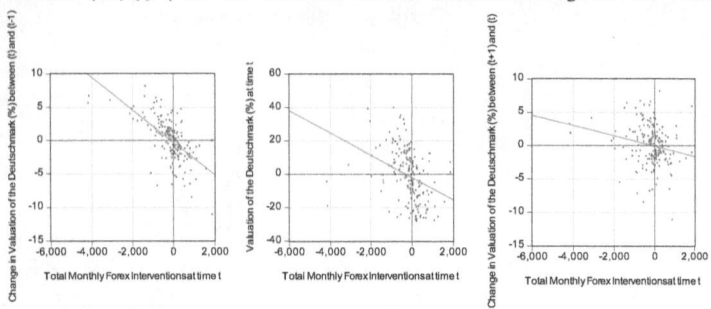

Figure 33: Scatterplot with red regression line of Nonzero Monthly German Forex Interventions against the U.S. under Karl Otto Pöhl, 1980:01-1991:07, in millions of Dollars measured at time t, against the respective % changes between (t)-(t-1) , the % level at (t) , and % changes between (t+1)-(t), in the Valuation of the Deutschmark against the Dollar.

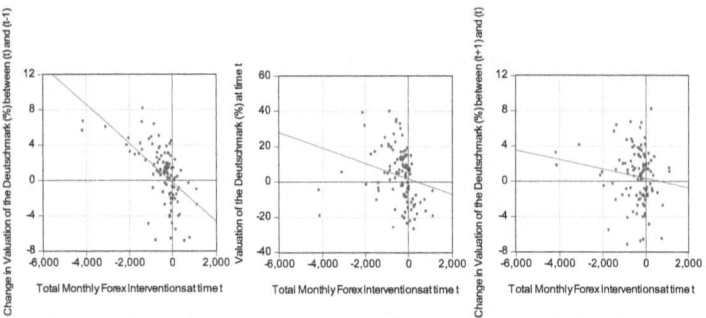

For Figure 34, I construct Real Exchange Rates for U.S.-Japan and U.S.-Germany by taking: $RER = e_{j,t} \left(\dfrac{p_t}{p_{j,t}} \right)$

Where the exchange rate is the nominal spot or forward rates and p are the respective CPI Indices.

Figure 34: Scatterplot with red regression line of Nonzero Bilateral Monthly G-3 Forex Interventions in Post Bretton Woods, 1973:03-2004:10, in millions of Dollars measured at time t, against % logarithmic changes, measured for (t+1)-(t) , of the 3-Month Nominal and Real Forward rates, and Nominal and Real Monthly-Average Spot rates of the corresponding G-3 Forex Markets; measure either in Yen/Dollar or Deutschmark/Dollar.

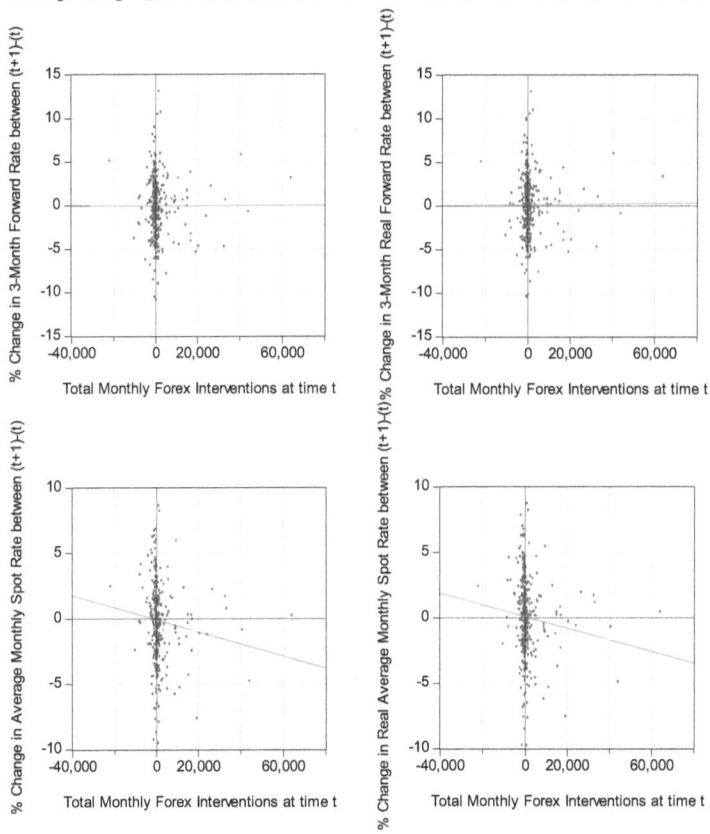

Figure 35: Scatterplot with red regression line of Nonzero Total Bilateral Monthly G-3 Forex Interventions under the Burns and Miller Fed, 1973:03-1979:07, in millions of Dollars measured at time t, against % logarithmic change, measured for (t+1)-(t) , of the 3-Month Real Forward rates and Real Monthly-Average Spot rates of the corresponding G-3 Forex Markets; measure either in Yen/Dollar or Deutschmark/Dollar.

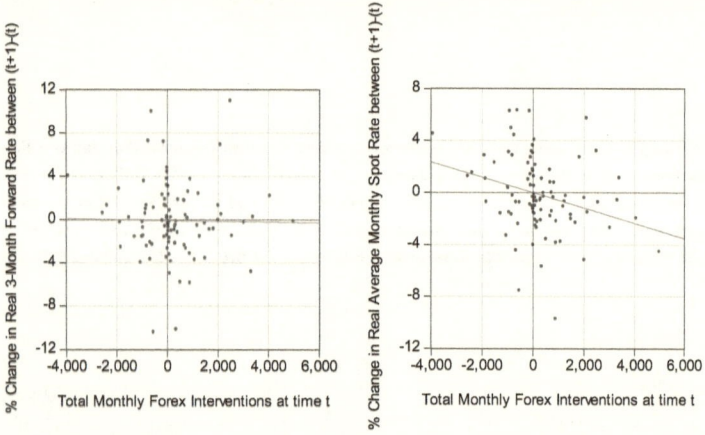

Figure 36: Scatterplot with red regression line of Nonzero Total Bilateral Monthly G-3 Forex Interventions under the Volcker Fed, 1979:08-1987:07, in millions of Dollars measured at time t, against % logarithmic change, measured for (t+1)-(t) , of the 3-Month Nominal Forward rates and Nominal Monthly-Average Spot rates of the corresponding G-3 Forex Markets; measure either in Yen/Dollar or Deutschmark/Dollar.

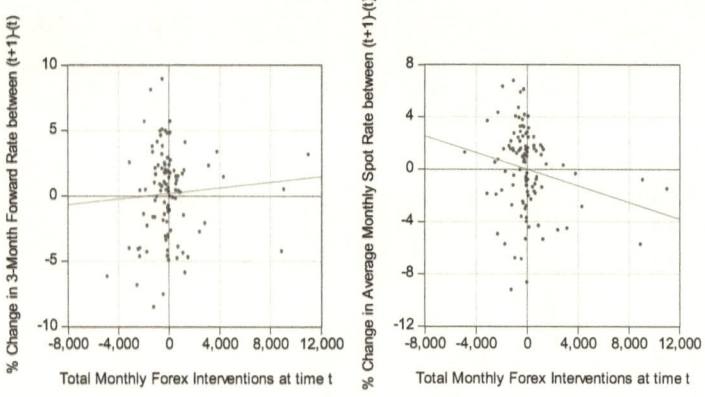

Figure 37: Scatterplot with red regression line of Nonzero Total Bilateral Monthly G-3 Forex Interventions under the Greenspan Fed, 1987:08-1995:12, in millions of Dollars measured at time t, against % logarithmic change, measured for (t+1)-(t) , of the 3-Month Real Forward rates and Nominal Monthly-Average Spot rates of the corresponding G-3

Forex Markets; measure either in Yen/Dollar or Deutschmark/Dollar.

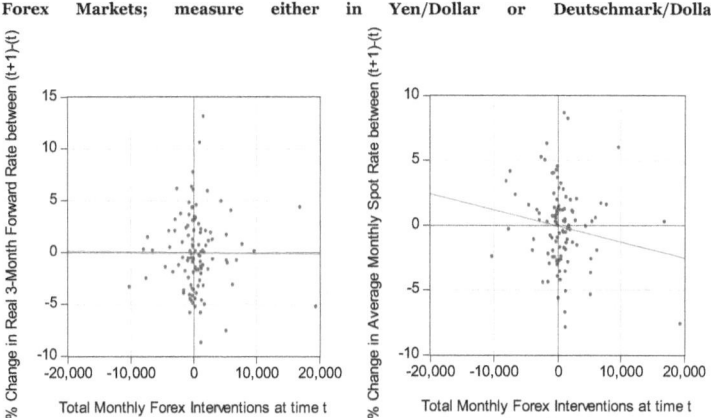

Figure 38: Scatterplot with red regression line of only Nonzero Monthly U.S. Forex Interventions against Japan and Germany under the Greenspan Fed, 1987:08-1995:12, in millions of Dollars measured at time t, against % logarithmic change, measured for (t+1)-(t) , of the 3-Month Nominal Forward rates and Real Monthly- Average Spot rates of the corresponding G-3 Forex Markets; measure either in Yen/Dollar or Deutschmark/Dollar.

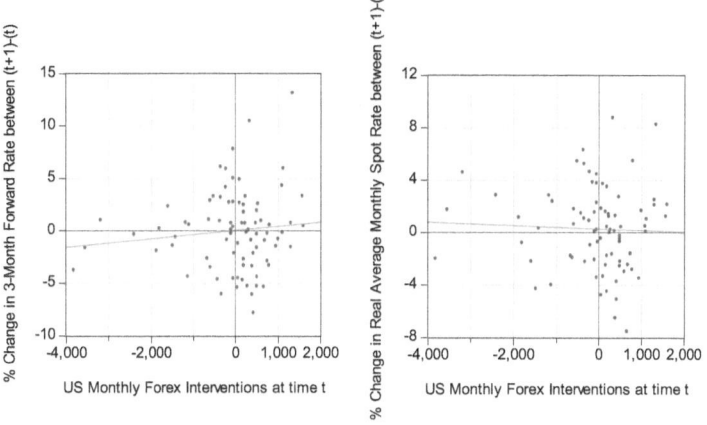

Figure 39: Scatterplot with red regression line of Nonzero Total Bilateral Monthly Japanese-U.S. Forex Interventions under the Japanese Interventionist period, 1991:04-2004:10, in millions of Dollars measured at time t, against % logarithmic change, measured for (t+1)-(t) , of the 3-Month Real Forward rates and Nominal Monthly-Average Spot Yen/Dollar rates.

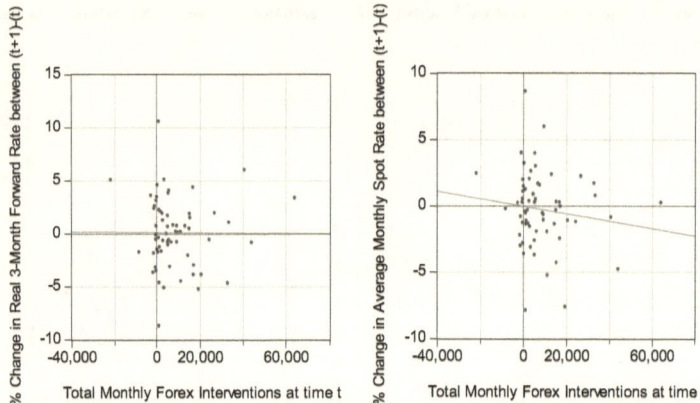

Figure 40: Scatterplot with red regression line of Nonzero Total Bilateral Monthly German-U.S. Forex Interventions under Karl Otto Pöhl, 1980:01-1991:07, in millions of Dollars measured at time t, against % logarithmic change, measured for (t+1)-(t), of the 3-Month Nominal Forward rates and Nominal Monthly- Average Spot Deutschmark/Dollar rates.

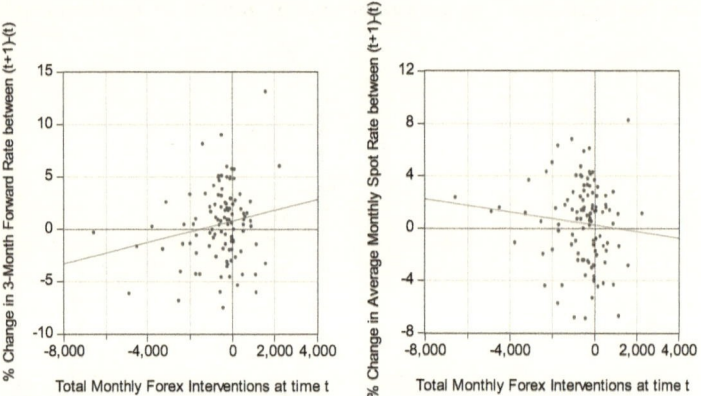

Finally, SVAR allows for making explicit identification assumptions to isolate policy behaviour and its effects on the economy whilst keeping the model free from restrictive assumptions otherwise needed to give every parameter a behavioural interpretation. An and Sun, in 'Monetary Policy, Foreign Exchange Intervention, and the Exchange Rate: The Case of Japan', said "a structural VAR model considering the unusual distribution of intervention could be more successful in identifying the policies". The relationships amongst macroeconomic variables can be modelled simply by the following

SVAR: $A_0 Y_t = A_1 Y_{t-1} + A_2 Y_{t-2} + ... + A_p Y_{t-p} + \varepsilon_t$

Where Y is a vector of endogenous components at time t, A is a matrix of parameters, and the multivariate white noise error process, which contains the following properties:

$E(\varepsilon_t) = 0$,

$E(\varepsilon_t \varepsilon'_t) = \begin{cases} \Sigma & t=\tau \\ 0 & \text{otherwise} \end{cases}$

The SVAR assumes that error processes are orthogonal, such that the structural disturbances are uncorrelated and the variance-covariance matrix is constant and diagonal; the contemporaneous matrix, A_0, is normalised across the main diagonal such that each equation in the SVAR system has a dependent variable; and the parameters are estimated in two stages. Firstly, to estimate the reduced form VAR of the SVAR:

$Y_t = A_0^{-1} A_1 Y_{t-1} + A_0^{-1} A_2 Y_{t-2} + ... + A_0^{-1} A_p Y_{t-p} + A_0^{-1} \varepsilon_t$

$Y_t = B_1 A_1 Y_{t-1} + B_2 A_2 Y_{t-2} + ... + B_p A_p Y_{t-p} + v_t$

Where $B_i = A_0^{-1} A_i$, $i=1,2,...p$ and $v_t = A_0^{-1} \varepsilon_t, v_t \sim N(0,\Omega)$. Structural Innovations are linked to the reduced form innovations from:

$$E(v_t v'_t) = A_0^{-1} (\varepsilon_t \varepsilon'_t) A_0^{-1'}$$

$$\Omega = A_0^{-1} \Sigma (A_0^{-1})'$$

And then secondly, to identify the contemporaneous matrix and the variance-covariance matrix which maximises the likelihood function conditional on the reduced form parameter estimates.

I identify the reactions of Interventions, Monetary Policy, and Exchange Rate within a unified structural model:

$$A_0 y_t = A(L) y_{t-1} + \varepsilon_t$$

A_0 is the contemporaneous coefficient matrix; $A(L)$ is a matrix polynomial in the lag operator L; y_t is an $n \times 1$ data vector.

I adapt the methodology from the literature by estimating an 'Absolute SVAR' consisting of Data vector:

$$y_t = [FEI, I, M, CPI, FFR, IP, Oil, E]$$

All Time Series for both Absolute and Relative SVAR for U.S., Japan, and Germany were stationary in their respective entered Format in the SVAR; following the rejection of the null hypothesis from the Augmented Dickey-Fuller Unit Root Test. FEI corresponds to Bilateral Monthly U.S.-Japanese, U.S.-German, and total G-3 Forex Interventions, converted into Billions of Dollars, for Japan, German, and U.S. Absolute SVAR, respectively; I are the Call Money Rates for Japan and Germany, and Bank Prime Loan Rate for the U.S.; M is M2 supply for Japan and the U.S., and M3 supply for Germany (The Bundesbank implicitly targeted the M3 measure for much of its Interventionist Period; and explicitly from 1987 onwards); CPI are U.S., German, and Japanese Consumer Price Indices; FFR stands for U.S. Federal Funds Rate; IP for U.S., German, and Japanese

Industrial Production; OIL for Oil price; E are Nominal Trade-weighted Dollar Index, Deutschmark/Dollar, Yen/Dollar for U.S., German, and Japan Absolute SVAR, respectively. In the entry format for the SVAR, all apart from FEI, I, and FFR, are entered as logarithms.

I apply the following non-recursive non-zero contemporaneous mapping of structural restrictions on the components of the Absolute Japanese and German SVAR:

$$\begin{bmatrix} 1 & g_{12} & 0 & 0 & 0 & 0 & 0 & g_{18} \\ 0 & 1 & g_{23} & 0 & 0 & g_{26} & g_{27} & g_{28} \\ 0 & g_{32} & 1 & g_{34} & g_{35} & 0 & 0 & 0 \\ 0 & 0 & 0 & 1 & g_{45} & 0 & g_{47} & 0 \\ 0 & 0 & 0 & 0 & 1 & 0 & g_{57} & 0 \\ 0 & g_{62} & 0 & 0 & 0 & 1 & g_{67} & 0 \\ 0 & 0 & 0 & 0 & 0 & 0 & 1 & 0 \\ g_{81} & g_{82} & g_{83} & g_{84} & g_{85} & g_{86} & g_{87} & 1 \end{bmatrix} \begin{bmatrix} FEI \\ I \\ M \\ CPI \\ IP \\ FFR \\ OIL \\ E \end{bmatrix} = A(L) \begin{bmatrix} FEI \\ I \\ M \\ CPI \\ IP \\ FFR \\ OIL \\ E \end{bmatrix} + \begin{bmatrix} \varepsilon_{FEI} \\ \varepsilon_{I} \\ \varepsilon_{M} \\ \varepsilon_{CPI} \\ \varepsilon_{IP} \\ \varepsilon_{FFR} \\ \varepsilon_{Oil} \\ \varepsilon_{e} \end{bmatrix}$$

And following mapping restrictions on the structure of the Absolute U.S. SVAR:

$$\begin{bmatrix} 1 & g_{12} & 0 & 0 & 0 & 0 & 0 & g_{18} \\ 0 & 1 & g_{23} & 0 & 0 & g_{26} & g_{27} & g_{28} \\ 0 & g_{32} & 1 & g_{34} & g_{35} & 0 & 0 & 0 \\ 0 & 0 & 0 & 1 & g_{45} & 0 & g_{47} & 0 \\ 0 & 0 & 0 & 0 & 1 & 0 & g_{57} & 0 \\ 0 & g_{62} & 0 & 0 & 0 & 1 & g_{67} & 0 \\ 0 & 0 & 0 & 0 & 0 & 0 & 1 & 0 \\ g_{81} & g_{82} & g_{83} & g_{84} & g_{85} & g_{86} & g_{87} & 1 \end{bmatrix} \begin{bmatrix} FEI \\ FFR \\ M \\ CPI \\ IP \\ I \\ OIL \\ E \end{bmatrix} = A(L) \begin{bmatrix} FEI \\ FFR \\ M \\ CPI \\ IP \\ I \\ OIL \\ E \end{bmatrix} + \begin{bmatrix} \varepsilon_{FEI} \\ \varepsilon_{FFR} \\ \varepsilon_{M} \\ \varepsilon_{CPI} \\ \varepsilon_{IP} \\ \varepsilon_{I} \\ \varepsilon_{Oil} \\ \varepsilon_{e} \end{bmatrix}$$

These yield the following results (** and * denotes if coefficients are significant at 5% or 10%, respectively).

Japanese Absolute SVAR:

$$\begin{bmatrix} 1 & -0.402031 & 0 & 0 & 0 & 0 & 0 & 1.649987^{**} \\ 0 & 1 & 46.49151 & 0 & 0 & 0.785511 & -0.005981 & -2.3174 \\ 0 & -5.373671 & 1 & -0.938942 & 0.127745 & 0 & 0 & 0 \\ 0 & 0 & 0 & 1 & -0.01184^{**} & 0 & -0.000525 & 0 \\ 0 & 0 & 0 & 0 & 1 & 0 & -0.02746 & 0 \\ 0 & -0.121072^{*} & 0 & 0 & 0 & 1 & -0.012655^{*} & 0 \\ 0 & 0 & 0 & 0 & 0 & 0 & 1 & 0 \\ -0.032354^{*} & -0.145021 & 6.624707^{*} & 0.443472^{*} & 0.065384^{*} & -0.354428^{**} & 0.029537^{*} & 1 \end{bmatrix}$$

German Absolute SVAR:

$$\begin{bmatrix} 1 & 0.049171 & 0 & 0 & 0 & 0 & 0 & 0.774256^{**} \\ 0 & 1 & -1.82646 & 0 & 0 & 0.172066^{*} & -0.00195 & -0.00482 \\ 0 & 0.215727^{*} & 1 & 0.239499^{**} & -0.00759 & 0 & 0 & 0 \\ 0 & 0 & 0 & 1 & 0.002945 & 0 & -0.00584^{**} & 0 \\ 0 & 0 & 0 & 0 & 1 & 0 & -0.03078^{**} & 0 \\ 0 & -0.19803 & 0 & 0 & 0 & 1 & -0.00393 & 0 \\ 0 & 0 & 0 & 0 & 0 & 0 & 1 & 0 \\ -0.66743^{*} & -0.37477 & -0.14264 & -0.63668 & -0.07995 & -0.62271^{**} & 0.004408 & 1 \end{bmatrix}$$

U.S. Absolute SVAR:

$$\begin{bmatrix} 1 & 0.34616^{*} & 0 & 0 & 0 & 0 & 0 & -1.325044^{**} \\ 0 & 1 & -2.804807^{*} & 0 & 0 & -0.472914^{*} & -0.016697 & 0.636957^{*} \\ 0 & 0.104601^{**} & 1 & -0.022308 & -0.102609^{**} & 0 & 0 & 0 \\ 0 & 0 & 0 & 1 & -0.025492^{*} & 0 & -0.007868^{**} & 0 \\ 0 & 0 & 0 & 0 & 1 & 0 & -0.005798 & 0 \\ 0 & -0.372915^{**} & 0 & 0 & 0 & 1 & -0.000243 & 0 \\ 0 & 0 & 0 & 0 & 0 & 0 & 1 & 0 \\ 0.041832 & -2.565585 & 7.084984^{*} & 0.988763 & 1.128224 & 2.459753 & 0.005087 & 1 \end{bmatrix}$$

The following are the separate Impulse Responses from these Absolute SVAR of notable Intervention Regimes.

Figure 41: Impulse Responses to U.S. policy shocks for Absolute SVAR under the Greenspan Fed, 1987:08- 1995:12. Additional Information: positive shocks in FEI, FFR, and E over 12 months with Monte-Carlo Simulation with 500 draws.

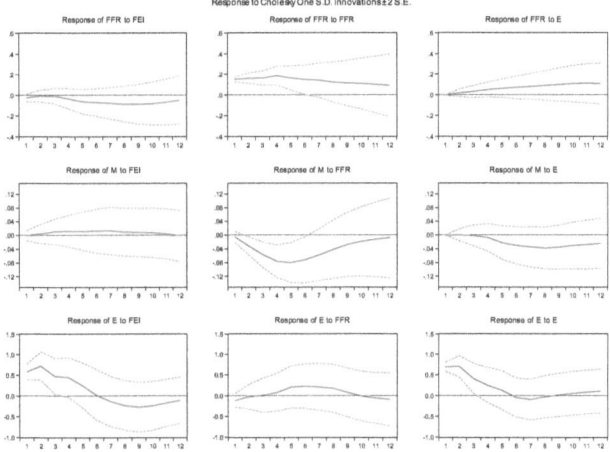

Figure 42: Impulse Responses to Japanese policy shocks in Absolute SVAR under the Japanese Interventionist Period, 1991:04-2004:10.

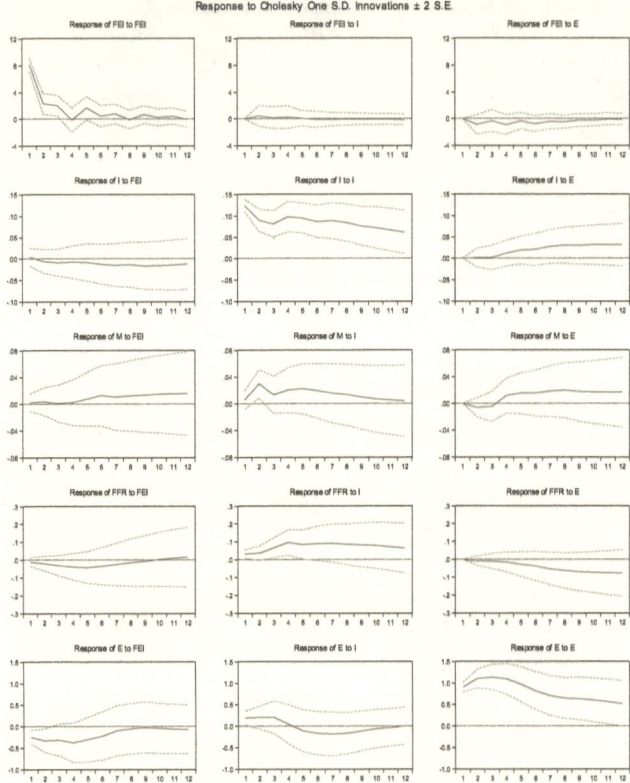

Figure 43: Impulse Responses to German policy shocks for Absolute SVAR under Karl Otto Pöhl, 1980:01- 1991:07.

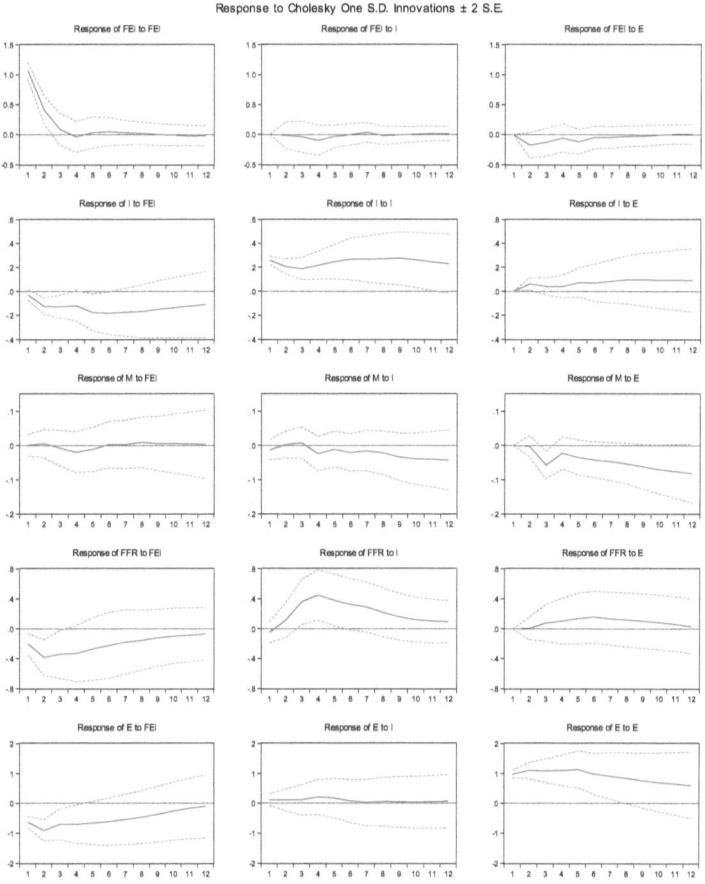

Additionally, I estimate a 'Relative SVAR' with relative components with monthly- frequency, four lags, Data vector y in:

$$A_0 y_t = A(L) y_{t-1} + \varepsilon_t$$

Which includes the following relative components (where for instance E is the % valuation):

$$[FEI, \ddddot{I}, \ddddot{M}, \ddddot{CPI}, \ddddot{IP}, Oil, \ddddot{E}]$$

I then apply the following non-recursive non-zero contemporaneous mapping of structural restrictions for the Japanese, German, and the U.S. Relative SVAR:

$$\begin{bmatrix} 1 & g_{12} & 0 & 0 & 0 & 0 & g_{17} \\ 0 & 1 & g_{23} & 0 & 0 & g_{26} & g_{27} \\ 0 & g_{32} & 1 & g_{34} & g_{35} & 0 & 0 \\ 0 & 0 & 0 & 1 & g_{45} & g_{46} & 0 \\ 0 & 0 & 0 & 0 & 1 & g_{56} & 0 \\ 0 & 0 & 0 & 0 & 0 & 1 & 0 \\ g_{71} & g_{72} & g_{73} & g_{74} & g_{75} & g_{76} & 1 \end{bmatrix} \begin{bmatrix} FEI \\ \ddddot{I} \\ \ddddot{M} \\ \ddddot{CPI} \\ \ddddot{IP} \\ OIL \\ \ddddot{E} \end{bmatrix} = A(L) \begin{bmatrix} FEI \\ \ddddot{I} \\ \ddddot{M} \\ \ddddot{CPI} \\ \ddddot{IP} \\ OIL \\ \ddddot{E} \end{bmatrix} + \begin{bmatrix} \varepsilon_{FEI} \\ \varepsilon_{\ddddot{I}} \\ \varepsilon_{\ddddot{M}} \\ \varepsilon_{\ddddot{CPI}} \\ \varepsilon_{\ddddot{IP}} \\ \varepsilon_{OIL} \\ \varepsilon_{\ddddot{E}} \end{bmatrix}$$

These yield following results; for Japanese Relative SVAR:

$$\begin{bmatrix} 1 & -0.18801 & 0 & 0 & 0 & 0 & 0.257995 \\ 0 & 1 & -4.10824* & 0 & 0 & 0.016155 & 0.028122 \\ 0 & 1.702258* & 1 & 0.128065 & -0.1573* & 0 & 0 \\ 0 & 0 & 0 & 1 & 0.021654 & 0.006547 & 0 \\ 0 & 0 & 0 & 0 & 1 & -0.01325 & 0 \\ 0 & 0 & 0 & 0 & 0 & 1 & 0 \\ 0.035563 & 0.276336 & 0.465305 & 0.359214** & 0.1205* & 0.045143 & 1 \end{bmatrix}$$

For German Relative SVAR:

$$\begin{bmatrix} 1 & -0.055123* & 0 & 0 & 0 & 0 & 0.132719** \\ 0 & 1 & -0.440192 & 0 & 0 & 0.032558* & 0.166253 \\ 0 & 0.156631 & 1 & 0.266424** & -0.002031 & 0 & 0 \\ 0 & 0 & 0 & 1 & -0.002277 & 0.001137 & 0 \\ 0 & 0 & 0 & 0 & 1 & -0.056683** & 0 \\ 0 & 0 & 0 & 0 & 0 & 1 & 0 \\ -1.134638 & -0.801205 & 0.44416 & 3.405096** & -0.031596 & -0.067545 & 1 \end{bmatrix}$$

For U.S.-Japan relative SVAR:

$$\begin{bmatrix} 1 & 0.056644 & 0 & 0 & 0 & 0 & -0.024727^{**} \\ 0 & 1 & -3.118697 & 0 & 0 & -0.014001 & -2.427933 \\ 0 & 0.092799 & 1 & 0.019722 & -0.016704 & 0 & 0 \\ 0 & 0 & 0 & 1 & 0.03267^{*} & 0.004329 & 0 \\ 0 & 0 & 0 & 0 & 1 & 0.009433 & 0 \\ 0 & 0 & 0 & 0 & 0 & 1 & 0 \\ -6.507024 & 18.47187 & -10.77801 & 1.317435 & -1.931732 & -0.198934 & 1 \end{bmatrix}$$

For U.S.- Germany relative SVAR:

$$\begin{bmatrix} 1 & -0.003572 & 0 & 0 & 0 & 0 & -0.090668^{**} \\ 0 & 1 & 1.665277^{*} & 0 & 0 & -0.025973 & -0.161909 \\ 0 & -0.369149 & 1 & 0.213127^{**} & 0.029054^{*} & 0 & 0 \\ 0 & 0 & 0 & 1 & 0.003409 & 0.000116 & 0 \\ 0 & 0 & 0 & 0 & 1 & 0.064676^{*} & 0 \\ 0 & 0 & 0 & 0 & 0 & 1 & 0 \\ 0.694239 & 1.321434^{*} & 1.233786 & 1.287867^{**} & -0.047091 & -0.035352 & 1 \end{bmatrix}$$

Figure 44: Impulse Responses to Japanese policy shocks in Relative SVAR, 1973:03-2004:10.

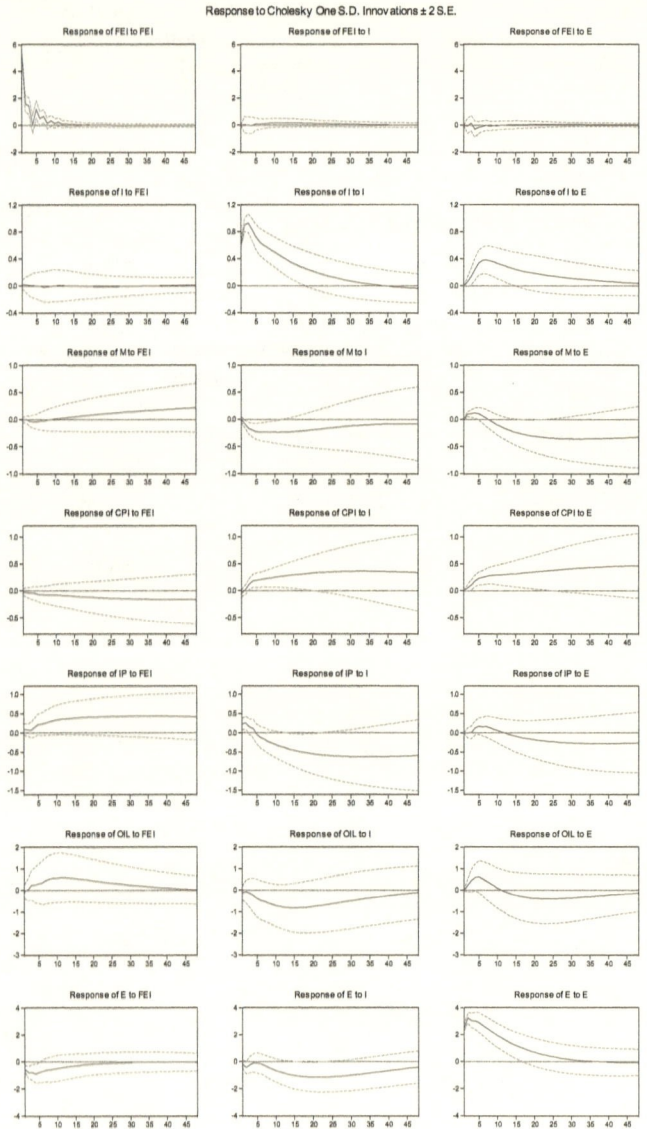

Figure 45: Impulse Responses to German policy shocks for Relative SVAR, 1973:03-1995:12.

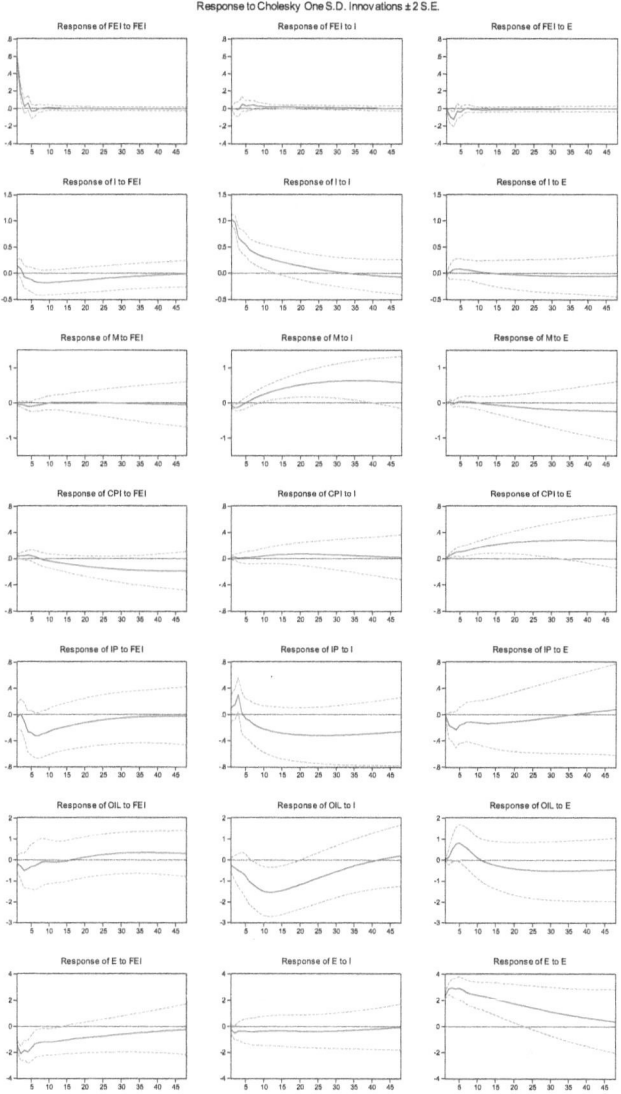

Figure 46: Impulse Responses to U.S. policy shocks for U.S.-Japan Relative SVAR, 1973:03-1995:12.

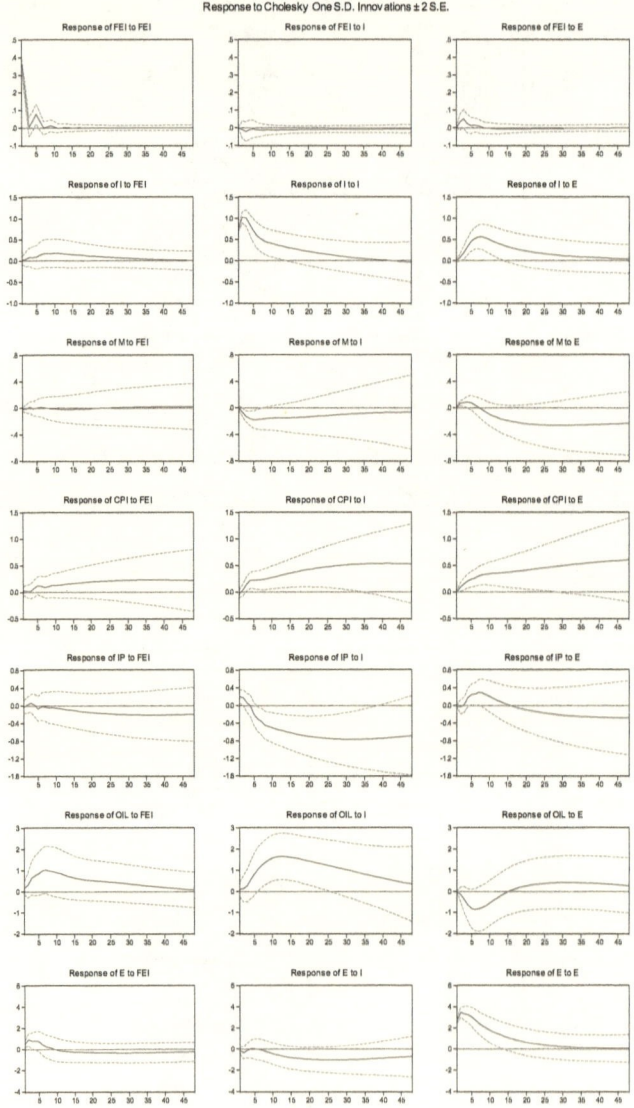

Figure 47: Impulse Responses to U.S. policy shocks for U.S.-Germany Relative SVAR, 1973:03-1995:12.

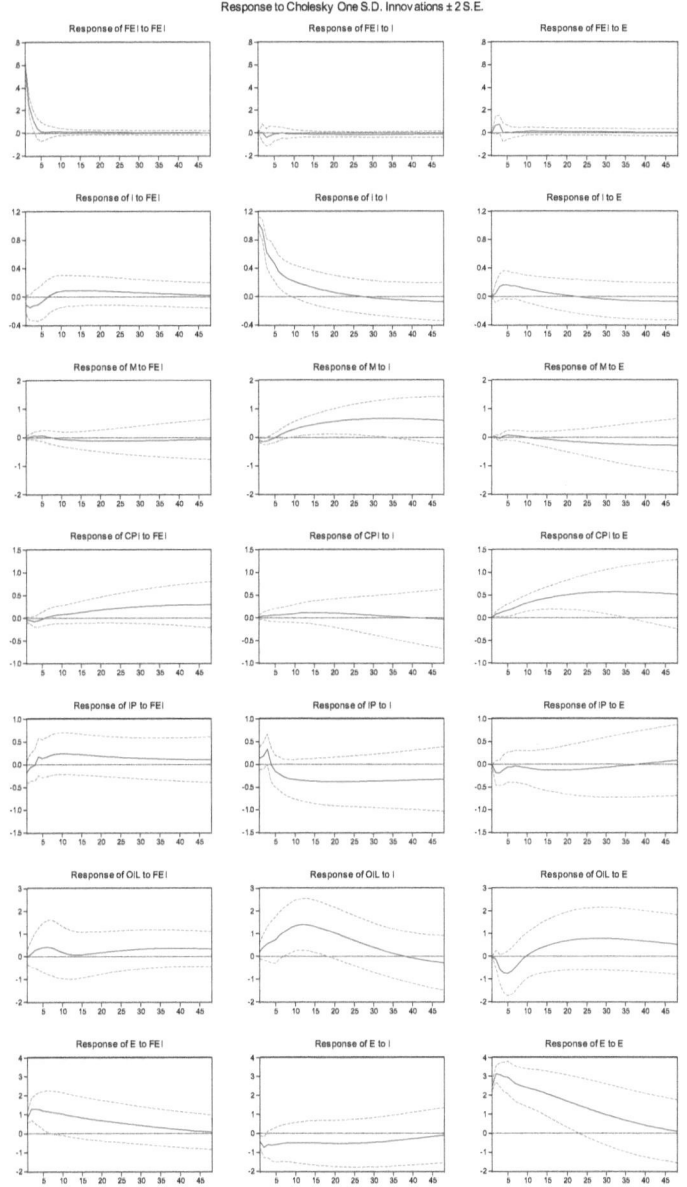

Chapter 8

"De Omnibus Dubitandum"

This book has covered a wide range by using an array of approaches from the narrative to the quantitative; correspondingly, I have charted the tumultuous nature of economic policy of Post Bretton Woods. In the methodology, I attempted to analyse different policy regimes and periods within specified frameworks. Given the breadth of models used, the empirical results are, at first glance, multi-dimensional.

For the Valuation Event studies, as a whole, suggest policymakers react to a negative change in valuation of their currencies by Intervening. The outcome for most is a successful decrease in the rate of the negative change in valuation as opposed to a level or rate reversal; Greenspan and Pöhl regimes do well under this study.

The ex post Event studies give mixed results. The Forward rate returns a more successful measure of Intervention success than the Spot. At the same time all regimes measured by the Spot rate had ambivalent success. This indicates private expectations may not be self-fulfilling. Reflecting a wider market inefficiency and 'momentum' and 'naive' forex trading conducted by private agents.

For all the Absolute SVAR, g_{18}, the reactiveness of Forex Interventions to exchange rate, was significant and with the correct sign. For the U.S. SVAR, the Fed Rate, g_{28}, is significantly responsive to the exchange-rate as well. The Impulse-responses for Intervention shocks on monetary policy weakly supports the signalling hypothesis; however, correct directional-movement of the exchange- rates in the first six months follows Intervention shocks. Reaction of exchange-rate to monetary policy shocks are varied supporting various Uncovered Interest Parity, 'overshooting', and 'delayed overshooting' hypotheses for Germany, Japan, and U.S., respectively. This corroborates the conflicts within the Uncovered Interest Parity literature first highlighted by Eichenbaum and Evans, in *'Some empirical evidence on the effects of monetary policy shocks on exchange rates'*, and Grilli and Roubini, *'Liquidity and Exchange Rates: Puzzling Evidence from the G-7 countries'*. The exchange-rate shocks on Interventions do not validate 'leaning-against-the-wind' policy but does so with monetary policy.

Variance-Decomposition for U.S. Monetary policy fluctuations has some attribution to exchange-rate shocks; whilst U.S. monetary policy shocks account for a significant amount of exchange-rate variance; 33.8% at the 48-month horizon is a far greater account of U.S. exchange rate variance than found by Kim, who actually estimated Interventions to have attributed a larger contribution to exchange rate fluctuation. Absolute SVAR were also re-estimated for notable policy regimes. Amongst them, Greenspan's Monetary and Intervention Policies were kept at an arm's length from each other, the latter had a significant impact on exchange rate, whilst the former made a large impact on money supply; suggesting Greenspan pursued two separate goals with two instruments.

The results for the Japanese Interventionist Period supports the Institutional disharmony, confirmed by the narrative between the Ministry of Finance and the Bank of Japan, and reflected foremost in the lack of immediacy of monetary policy to exchange rate shocks in the impulse-responses. Whereas, Pöhl's monetary policy was collaborative with forthcoming unilateral German Interventions.

The Relative SVAR accounts for the mutual dependency of the components of Intervention modelling. Reactions of Interventions to exchange-rate valuation in g_{17} are significant and 'leaning-against-the-wind' for U.S. and Germany. Impulse-responses of Exchange-rate valuation in the Relative SVAR to Intervention lead to the correct directional movement, albeit more pronounced for the U.S. and Germany. For the latter, the signalling mechanism of a supportive relative-monetary policy is also observable. Relative Interest-rate differentials between U.S. and Japan accentuate the monetary methods of addressing Yen and Dollar undervaluation shocks.

Decomposing U.S.-Japan Relative SVAR shows the significant variance attributed by exchange-rate valuation movements towards relative U.S.-Japanese monetary policies; similarly relative monetary policy has a significant hold over exchange-rate fluctuations. German Interventions account, to a large extent, for its exchange-rate valuation movements.

In summary, Exchange-rate stability under a full embrace of the Macroeconomic trinity is a chimera. However, Policymakers unfortunately seldom learn their lessons. Interventions may have been more effective if they were preceded by compatible monetary policy actions but that would assume Institutional harmony within the nexus of policymaking. Nevertheless, Interventions did spur bona fide policy coordination in late Post Bretton Woods. Additionally a paradigm shift was required to overcome the entrenched Interventionist Interests, which was only possible during Volcker and Greenspan Regimes for the U.S. Volcker's role in changing policy over U.S. Forex Interventions—initially to boost the Dollar in 1979 and then to reduce it following Plaza—cannot be understated. Intervention policy in Post Bretton Woods is a prism through which to view the evolution of exchange rates, as well as global economic policy. However throughout these chapters the leitmotif has been Interventions are a serious misallocation of resources and such is the described narrative within this book of its untended consequences, motivations for Forex Interventions are surrounded by the maxim *De Omnibus Dubitandum*.

References

All graphs, tables, and diagrams were created and designed by the Author and data files are available upon written request. All cited FOMC Transcripts, FOMC Memoranda of Discussions, Federal Reserve Bulletins, and Economic Reports of the President are available at Federal Reserve Archival System for Economic Research—FRASER—, Federal Reserve Board of St. Louis.

Primary References:

[1] Adams, D. and Henderson, D., 'Definition and Measurement of Exchange Market Intervention', Board of Governors of the Federal Reserve System, Staff Study 126 (1983).
[2] 'Announcement of the Ministers of Finance and Central Bank Governors of France, Germany, Japan, the United Kingdom, and the United States, 22nd September 1985', in Funabashi, Y., Managing the Dollar: From the Plaza to the Louvre (Washington D.C., 1989), pp. 261-266.
[3] Bank of Japan, 'List of Governors'
[4] Bank of Japan Act, 18th June 1997 .

[5] Bloomberg Businessweek, 'A Bold Campaign to end Endaka', 27th August 1995 (http://www.businessweek.com/stories/1995-08-27/a-bold-campaign-to-end-endaka-intl-edition).

[6] Cross, S., 'Treasury and Federal Reserve Foreign Exchange Operations', Federal Reserve Bank of New York Quarterly Review, Winter (1985-1986), pp. 45-48.

[7] Deutsche Bundesbank, 'Presidents Gallery'

[8] Deutsche Bundesbank Monthly Report, January 1995 (Deutsche Bundesbank, Frankfurt am Main).

[9] Deutsche Bundesbank Monthly Report, September 1995 (Deutsche Bundesbank, Frankfurt am Main).

[10] Economic Report of the President, January 1979, (The Council of Economic Advisers, Washington D.C.).

[11] Federal Reserve Board, 'Membership of the Board of Governors of the Federal Reserve System, 1914-Present'

[12] Federal Reserve Bulletin, December 1977 (Board of Governors of the Federal Reserve System, Washington D.C.).

[13] Federal Reserve Bulletin, January 1978 (Board of Governors of the Federal Reserve System, Washington D.C.).

[14] Federal Reserve Bulletin, March 1978 (Board of Governors of the Federal Reserve System, Washington D.C.).

[15] Federal Reserve Bulletin, September 1979 (Board of Governors of the Federal Reserve System, Washington D.C.).

[16] Federal Reserve Bulletin, June 1980 (Board of Governors of the Federal Reserve System, Washington D.C.).

[17] Federal Reserve Bulletin, November 1983 (Board of Governors of the Federal Reserve System, Washington D.C.).

[18] Federal Reserve Bulletin, February 1986 (Board of Governors of the Federal Reserve System, Washington D.C.).

[19] Federal Reserve Bulletin, May 1986 (Board of Governors of the Federal Reserve System, Washington D.C.).

[20] Federal Reserve Bulletin, October 1987 (Board of Governors of the Federal Reserve System, Washington D.C.).

[21] Federal Reserve Bulletin, January 1988 (Board of Governors of the Federal Reserve System, Washington D.C.).

[22] Federal Reserve Bulletin, April 1988 (Board of Governors of the Federal Reserve System, Washington D.C.).

[23] Federal Reserve Bulletin, October 1995 (Board of Governors of the Federal Reserve System, Washington D.C.).

[24] Foreign Exchange and Foreign Trade Act, 1st December 1949

[25] 'G-6 Communique, 22nd February 1987', in Funabashi, Y., Managing the Dollar: From the Plaza to the Louvre (Washington D.C., 1989), pp. 279-280.

[26] Greene, M., 'U.S. Experience with Exchange Market Intervention: January-March 1975', Board of Governors of the Federal Reserve System, Staff Study 127 (1984).

[27] Greene, M., 'U.S. Experience with Exchange Market Intervention: September 1977-December 1979' Board of Governors of the Federal Reserve System, Staff Study 128 (1984).

[28] Greene, M., 'U.S. Experience with Exchange Market Intervention: October 1980-September 1981' Board of Governors of the Federal Reserve System, Staff Study 129 (1984).

[29] Hayami, M., 'Getting down to work on reducing the surplus', Economic Eye, 14 (1993), pp. 4-7.

[30] Jurgensen, P., apport du roupe de travail sur les interventions sur les march s des changes [Report
of the Working Group on Exchange Market Intervention] (Paris, 1983).

[31] Los Angeles Times, 22nd March 1986

[32] Memorandum of Discussion of Federal Open Market Committee Meeting, 7th March 1973 (Board of Governors of the Federal Reserve System, Washington D.C.).

[33] Memorandum of Discussion of Federal Open Market Committee Meeting, 20th March 1973 (Board of Governors of the Federal Reserve System, Washington D.C.).

[34] Memorandum of Discussion of Federal Open Market Committee Meeting, 9th July 1973 (Board of Governors of the Federal Reserve System, Washington D.C.).

[35] Memorandum of Discussion of Federal Open Market Committee Meeting, 19th November 1973 (Board of Governors of the Federal Reserve System, Washington D.C.).

[36] Memorandum of Discussion of Federal Open Market Committee Meeting, 15th July 1975 (Board of Governors of the Federal Reserve System, Washington D.C.).

[37] Memorandum of Discussion of Federal Open Market Committee Meeting, 16th December 1975 (Board of Governors of the Federal Reserve System, Washington D.C.).

[38] Monatsberichte der Deutschen Bundesbank, February 1988 (Deutsche Bundesbank, Frankfurt Am Main).

[39] Monthly Economic Review, 19th November 1993 (Bank of Japan, Tokyo).

[40] Monthly Economic Review, 19th September 1995 (Bank of Japan, Tokyo).

[41] Monthly Report of the Deutsche Bundesbank, March 1973 (Deutsche Bundesbank, Frankfurt am Main).

[42] Monthly Report of the Deutsche Bundesbank, June 1975 (Deutsche Bundesbank, Frankfurt am Main).

[43] Monthly Report of the Deutsche Bundesbank, March 1976 (Deutsche Bundesbank, Frankfurt am Main).

[44] Monthly Report of the Deutsche Bundesbank, November 1978 (Deutsche Bundesbank, Frankfurt am Main).

[45] Monthly Report of the Deutsche Bundesbank, September 1979 (Deutsche Bundesbank, Frankfurt am Main).

[46] Monthly Report of the Deutsche Bundesbank, November 1979 (Deutsche Bundesbank, Frankfurt am Main).

[47] Monthly Report of the Deutsche Bundesbank, December 1979 (Deutsche Bundesbank, Frankfurt am Main).

[48] Monthly Report of the Deutsche Bundesbank, February 1981(Deutsche Bundesbank, Frankfurt am Main).

[49] Monthly Report of the Deutsche Bundesbank, January 1987 (Deutsche Bundesbank, Frankfurt am Main).

[50] Monthly Report of the Deutsche Bundesbank, February 1987 (Deutsche Bundesbank, Frankfurt am Main).

[51] Monthly Report of the Deutsche Bundesbank, February 1988 (Deutsche Bundesbank, Frankfurt am Main).

[52] Monthly Report of the Deutsche Bundesbank, November 1988 (Deutsche Bundesbank, Frankfurt am Main).

[53] Monthly Report of the Deutsche Bundesbank, February 1989 (Deutsche Bundesbank, Frankfurt am Main).

[54] Monthly Report of the Deutsche Bundesbank, February 1990 (Deutsche Bundesbank, Frankfurt am Main).

[55] Monthly Report of the Deutsche Bundesbank, December 1990 (Deutsche Bundesbank, Frankfurt am Main).

[56] Monthly Report of the Deutsche Bundesbank, September 1992 (Deutsche Bundesbank, Frankfurt am Main).

[57] Monthly Report of the Deutsche Bundesbank, October 1992 (Deutsche Bundesbank, Frankfurt am Main).

[58] Monthly Report of the Deutsche Bundesbank, December 1992 (Deutsche Bundesbank, Frankfurt am Main).

[59] Nippon Credit Bank, Survey Japan, August 1993.

[60] Prime Minister of Japan and his Cabinet, 'Previous Cabinets'

[61] Quarterly Economic Outlook, Summer 1986, Bank of Japan Special Paper 141.

[62] Quarterly Economic Outlook, Winter 1986, Bank of Japan Special Paper 146.

[63] Quarterly Economic Outlook, Winter 1988, Bank of Japan Special Paper 158.

[64] Quarterly Economic Outlook, Winter 1990, Bank of Japan Special Paper 185.

[65] Quarterly Economic Outlook, Autumn 1992, Bank of Japan Special Paper 222.

[66] Report of the Deutsche Bundesbank, 1973 (Deutsche Bundesbank, Frankfurt am Main).

[67] Report of the Deutsche Bundesbank, 1974 (Deutsche Bundesbank, Frankfurt am Main).

[68] Report of the Deutsche Bundesbank, 1975 (Deutsche Bundesbank, Frankfurt am Main).

[69] Report of the Deutsche Bundesbank, 1977 (Deutsche Bundesbank, Frankfurt am Main).

[70] Report of the Deutsche Bundesbank, 1978 (Deutsche Bundesbank, Frankfurt am Main).

[71] Report of the Deutsche Bundesbank, 1979 (Deutsche Bundesbank, Frankfurt am Main).

[72] Report of the Deutsche Bundesbank, 1981 (Deutsche Bundesbank, Frankfurt am Main).

[73] Report of the Deutsche Bundesbank, 1983 (Deutsche Bundesbank, Frankfurt am Main).

[74] Report of the Deutsche Bundesbank, 1984 (Deutsche Bundesbank, Frankfurt am Main).

[75] Report of the Deutsche Bundesbank, 1987 (Deutsche Bundesbank, Frankfurt am Main).

[76] Sakakibara, E., The day Japan and the world shuddered: establishment of cyber-capitalism (Tokyo, 2000).

[77] The Economist, 22nd November 1975.

[78] The Economist, 28th October 1978.

[79] The Economist, 28th April 1979.

[80] The Economist, 20th June 1987.

[81] The Economist, 24th September 1988.

[82] The Economist, 27th April 1991.

[83] The Economist, 27th July 1991.

[84] The Economist, 14th May 1994.

[85] The Economist, 23rd September 1995.

[86] The Economist, 7th October 1995.

[87] The Financial Times, 3rd June 1982.

[88] The Financial Times, 23rd March 1988.

[89] The Financial Times, 13th February 1993.

[90] The Financial Times, 10th March 1995.

[91] The Financial Times, 23rd January 1998.

[92] The Financial Times, 6th August 2003.

[93] The FT Review of Business Books, 23rd September 1993.

[94] The New York Times, 16th September 1995

[95] The Nikkei Weekly, Japan Economic Almanac 1988 (Tokyo 1988).

[96] The Nikkei Weekly, Japan Economic Almanac 1992 (Tokyo 1992).

[97] The Nikkei Weekly, Japan Economic Almanac 1997 (Tokyo 1997).

[98] The Nikkei Weekly, Japan Economic Almanac 1998 (Tokyo 1998).

[99] The Wall Street Journal, 4th September 1981.

[100] The Wall Street Journal, 8th August 2000.

[101] Time, 'Iran: Another Crisis for the Shah', 13th November 1978.

[102] Transcript of Federal Open Market Committee Meeting, 5th January 1978 (Board of Governors of the
Federal Reserve System, Washington D.C.).

[103] Transcript of Federal Open Market Committee Meeting, 17th January 1978 (Board of Governors of the
Federal Reserve System, Washington D.C.).

[104] Transcript of Federal Open Market Committee Meeting, 28th February 1978 (Board of Governors of
the Federal Reserve System, Washington D.C.).

[105] Transcript of Federal Open Market Committee Meeting, 21st March 1978 (Board of Governors of the Federal Reserve System, Washington D.C.).

[106] Transcript of Federal Open Market Committee Meeting, 18th July 1978 (Board of Governors of the
Federal Reserve System, Washington D.C.).

[107] Transcript of Federal Open Market Committee Meeting, 17th July 1979 (Board of Governors of the
Federal Reserve System, Washington D.C.).

[108] Transcript of Federal Open Market Committee Meeting, 29th-30th March 1982 (Board of Governors of
the Federal Reserve System, Washington D.C.).

[109] Transcript of Federal Open Market Committee Meeting, 28th-29th March 1983 (Board of Governors of
the Federal Reserve System, Washington D.C.).

[110] Transcript of Federal Open Market Committee Meeting, 19th-20th December 1983 (Board of Governors

of the Federal Reserve System, Washington D.C.).

[111] Transcript of Federal Open Market Committee Meeting, 16th-17th December 1985 (Board of Governors of the Federal Reserve System, Washington D.C.).

[112] Transcript of Federal Open Market Committee Meeting, 11th-12th February 1986 (Board of Governors of the Federal Reserve System, Washington D.C.).

[113] Transcript of Federal Open Market Committee Meeting, 19th August 1986 (Board of Governors of the Federal Reserve System, Washington D.C.).

[114] Transcript of Federal Open Market Committee Meeting, 3rd November 1987 (Board of Governors of the Federal Reserve System, Washington D.C.).

[115] Transcript of Federal Open Market Committee Meeting, 29th-30th June 1988 (Board of Governors of the Federal Reserve System, Washington D.C.).

[116] Transcript of Federal Open Market Committee Meeting, 16th August 1988 (Board of Governors of the Federal Reserve System, Washington D.C.).

[117] Transcript of Federal Open Market Committee Meeting, 1st November 1988 (Board of Governors of the Federal Reserve System, Washington D.C.).

[118] Transcript of Federal Open Market Committee Meeting, 16th May 1989 (Board of Governors of the Federal Reserve System, Washington D.C.).

[119] Transcript of Federal Open Market Committee Meeting, 5th-6th July 1989 (Board of Governors of the Federal Reserve System, Washington D.C.).

[120] Transcript of Federal Open Market Committee Meeting, 22nd August 1989 (Board of Governors of the Federal Reserve System, Washington D.C.).

[121] Transcript of Federal Open Market Committee Meeting, 3rd October 1989 (Board of Governors of the Federal Reserve System, Washington D.C.).

[122] Transcript of Federal Open Market Committee Meeting, 27th March 1990 (Board of Governors of the Federal Reserve System, Washington D.C.).

[123] Transcript of Federal Open Market Committee Meeting, 11th April 1990 (Board of Governors of the Federal Reserve System, Washington D.C.).

[124] Transcript of Federal Open Market Committee Meeting, 18th December 1990 (Board of Governors of the Federal Reserve System, Washington D.C.).

[125] Transcript of Federal Open Market Committee Meeting, 26th March 1991 (Board of Governors of the Federal Reserve System, Washington D.C.).

[126] Transcript of Federal Open Market Committee Meeting, 18th August 1992 (Board of Governors of the Federal Reserve System, Washington D.C.).

[127] Transcript of Federal Open Market Committee Meeting, 6th October 1992 (Board of Governors of the Federal Reserve System, Washington D.C.).

[128] Transcript of Federal Open Market Committee Meeting, 5th-6th July 1994 (Board of Governors of the Federal Reserve System, Washington D.C.).

[129] Transcript of Federal Open Market Committee Meeting, 15th November 1994 (Board of Governors of the Federal Reserve System, Washington D.C.).

[130] Transcript of Federal Open Market Committee Meeting, 28th March 1995 (Board of Governors of the Federal Reserve System, Washington D.C.).

[131] Transcript of Federal Open Market Committee Meeting, 22nd August 1995 (Board of Governors of the Federal Reserve System, Washington D.C.).

[132] Transcript of Federal Open Market Committee Meeting, 19th December 1995 (Board of Governors of the Federal Reserve System, Washington D.C.).

[133] Transcript of Federal Open Market Committee Meeting, 2nd-3rd July 1996 (Board of Governors of the Federal Reserve System, Washington D.C.).

[134] Transcript of Federal Open Market Committee Meeting, 29th-30th June 1999 (Board of Governors of the Federal Reserve System, Washington D.C.).

[135] Transcript of Federal Open Market Committee Meeting, 3rd October 2000 (Board of Governors of the Federal Reserve System, Washington D.C.).

[136] Transcript of Federal Open Market Committee Meeting, 30th-31st January 2001 (Board of Governors of the Federal Reserve System, Washington D.C.).

[137] U.S. Treasury, 'Secretaries of the Treasury'

[138] Volcker, P., 'Priorities for the International Monetary System', Federal Reserve Bank of New York, 17th November 1975

[139] Volcker, P. and Gyohten, T., Changing Fortunes, The World's Money and the Threat to American Leadership (New York, 1992).

[140] White House, 'The Presidents'

Secondary References:

[1]Adler, G. and Tovar, C., 'Foreign Exchange Intervention: A Shield Against Appreciation Winds?', International Monetary Fund, IMF Working Paper 165 (2011).

[2] Almekinders, G., Foreign Exchange Intervention: theory and evidence, (Cheltenham, 1993).

[3] An, L., and Sun, W., 'Monetary Policy, Foreign Exchange Intervention, and the Exchange Rate: The Case of Japan', International Research Journal of Finance and Economics, 15 (2008), pp. 271-283.

[4] Baille, R., Humpage, O., and Osterberg, W., 'Intervention from an Information perspective', Journal of International Financial Markets, Institutions and Money, 10 (2000), pp. 407-421.

[5] Baille, R. and Osterberg, W., 'Why do Central Banks Intervene?', Journal of International Money and Finance, 16 (1997), pp. 909-919.

[6] Beine, M., Grauwe, P., and Grimaldi, M., 'The Impact of FX Central Bank Intervention in a Noise Trading Framework', Journal of Banking & Finance, 33 (2009), pp. 1187-1195.

[7] Beine, M., Laurent, S., and Palm, F., 'Central Bank FOREX Interventions assessed using realized moments', Journal of International Financial Markets, Institutions and Money, 19 (2009), pp. 112-127.

[8] Bell, L., 'Ben Bernanke and the Zero Bound', The National Bureau of Economic Research, NBER Working Paper 17836 (2012).

[9] Bernal, O. and Gnabo, J., 'Announcements, financial operations or both? Generalizing central banks' FX reaction functions', Journal of the Japanese and International Economies, 23 (2009), pp. 367-394.

[10] Bhattacharya, U. and Weller, P., 'The Advantage of Hiding One's Hand: Speculation and Central Bank

Intervention in the Foreign Exchange Market', Journal of Monetary Economics, 39 (1997), pp. 251-277.

[11] Bofinger, 'The scope for Foreign Exchange Market Intervention', United Nations Conference on Trade
and Development, UNCTAD Discussion Paper 204 (2011).

[12] Bonser-Neal, C. and Tanner, G., 'Central bank intervention and the volatility of foreign exchange rates:
evidence from the options market', Federal Reserve Bank of Kansas City, Research Working Paper 4 (1995).

[13] Bordo, M., Humpage, O., and Schwartz, A., [BHS] 'Epilogue: Foreign Exchange Market Operations in
the Twenty First Century', Federal Reserve Bank of Cleveland, Working Paper 7 (2012).

[14] Bordo, M., Humpage, O., and Schwartz, A., [BHS] 'Foreign-exchange Intervention and the
Fundamental Trilemma of International Finance', VoxEU, 18th June 2012

[15] Bordo, M., Humpage, O., and Schwartz, A., [BHS], 'On the evolution of U.S. Foreign-Exchange Intervention: Thesis, Theory, and Institutions', Federal Reserve Bank of Cleveland, Working Paper 13 (2011).

[16] Bordo, M., Humpage, O., and Schwartz, A., [BHS] 'The Federal Reserve as an informed Foreign- Exchange Trader: 1973-1995', Federal Reserve Bank of Cleveland, Working Paper 18 (2011).

[17] Bordo, M., Humpage, O., and Schwartz, A., [BHS] 'U.S. Foreign-Exchange-Market Intervention during the Volcker-Greenspan Era', Federal Reserve Bank of Cleveland, Working Paper 7 (2010).

[18] Bordo, M., Humpage, O., and Schwartz, A., [BHS] 'U.S. Intervention and the early Dollar Float: 1973- 1981', Federal Reserve Bank of Cleveland, Working Paper 23 (2010).

[19] Chaboud, A. and Humpage, O., 'An Assessment of the Impact of Japanese Foreign Exchange Intervention: 1991-2004', Board of Governors of the Federal Reserve System, International Finance Discussion Paper 824 (2005).

[20] Cheung, Y. and Chinn, M., 'Currency Traders and Exchange Rate Dynamics: A Survey of the U.S. Market', Centre for Economic Studies, CESifo Working Paper 251 (2000).

[21] Destler, I. and Henning, C., Dollar Politics: Exchange Rate Policymaking in the United States (Washington D.C., 1989).

[22] Dominguez, K., 'Central bank intervention and exchange rate volatility', Journal of International Money and Finance, 17 (1998), pp. 161-190.

[23] Dominguez, K., 'The Market Microstructure of Central Bank Intervention', Journal of International Economics, 59 (2003), pp. 25-45.

[24] Dominguez, K., 'Market Responses to Coordinated Central Bank Intervention', Carnegie-Rochester Conference Series on Public Policy, 32 (1990), pp. 121-164.

[25] Dominguez, K., 'When do central bank interventions influence intra-daily and longer-term exchange rate movements?', Journal of International Money and Finance, 25 (2006), pp. 1051-1071.

[26] Dominguez, K. and Frankel, J., 'Does Foreign Exchange Intervention matter? The Portfolio Effect', American Economic Review, 83 (1993), pp. 1356-1369.

[27] Dominguez, K. and Frankel, J., Does Foreign Exchange Intervention Work? (Washington D.C., 1993).

[28] Dominguez, K. and Frankel, J., 'Foreign Exchange Intervention: an empirical assessment', in Frankel,

J., ed., On Exchange Rates (Cambridge, MA., 1993), pp. 327-345.

[29] Dominguez, K., 'Market Responses to Coordinated Central Bank Intervention', Carnegie-Rochester

Conference Series on Public Policy, 32 (1990), pp. 121-164.

[30] Edison,H., 'The effectiveness of central bank intervention: a survey of the literature after 1982', Department of Economics, Princeton University, Special Papers in International Economics 18 (1993).

[31] Eichenbaum, M. and Evans, C., 'Some empirical evidence on the effects of monetary policy shocks on exchange rates', Quarterly Journal of Economics, 110 (1995), pp. 975-1010.

[32] Engel, C., Mark, N., and West, K., 'Exchange Rate Models are not as bad as you think', The National Bureau of Economic Research, NBER Working Paper 13318 (2007).

[33] Engel, C. and West, K., 'Exchange Rates and fundamentals', The National Bureau of Economic Research, NBER Working Paper 10723 (2004).

[34] Evans, M. and Lyons, R., 'Are Different Currency Assets Imperfect Substitutes?', Centre for Economic Studies, CESifo Working Paper 978 (2003).

[35] Evans, M. and Lyons, R., 'Portfolio Balance, Price Impact, and Secret Intervention', The National Bureau of Economic Research, NBER Working Paper 8865 (2001).

[36] Fatum, R. and Hutchison, M., 'Effectiveness of official daily foreign exchange market intervention operations in Japan', The National Bureau of Economic Research, NBER Working Paper 9648 (2003).

[37] Fatum, R. and Hutchison, M., 'Evaluating foreign exchange market intervention: Self-selection, counterfactuals and average treatment effects', Journal of International Money and Finance, 29 (2010), pp. 570-584.

[38] Fatum, R. and Hutchison, M., 'Is Intervention a Signal of Future Monetary Policy?', Journal of Money, Credit and Banking, 31 (1999), pp. 54-69.

[39] Fatum, R. and Hutchison, M., 'Is Sterilized Foreign Exchange Intervention Effective after All?', The Economic Journal, 113 (2003), pp. 390-411.

[40] Fatum, R. and Yamamoto, Y., 'Does Foreign Exchange Volume matter?', Federal Reserve Bank of Dallas, Working Paper 115 (2012).

[41] Flood, R. and Marion, N., 'Self-fulfilling Risk Predictions: An Application to Speculative Attacks', Journal of International Economics, 50 (2000), pp. 245-268.

[42] Flood, R. and Rose, A., 'Fixing Exchange Rates: A virtual quest for fundamentals', Journal of Monetary Economics, 36 (1995), pp. 3-37.

[43] Frankel, J., Bergsten, C., and Mussa, M., 'Exchange Rate Policy', in Feldstein, ed., American Economic Policy in the 1980s (Chicago, 1994), pp. 293-366.

[44] Frenkel, M., Pierdzioch, C., and Stadtmann, G., 'The effects of Japanese foreign exchange market intervention on the Yen/U.S. Dollar exchange rate volatility', Kiel Institute for the World Economy, Kiel Working Paper 1165 (2003).

[45] Fratzscher, M., 'Exchange Rate Policy Strategies and Foreign Exchange Interventions in the Group of Three Economies', in Bergsten, C. and Williamson, J., eds., Dollar Adjustment: How far? Against what? (Washington D.C., 2004), pp. 259-271.

[46] Funabashi, Y., Managing the Dollar: From the Plaza to the Louvre (Washington D.C., 1989).

[47] Grilli, V. and Roubini, N., 'Liquidity and Exchange Rates: Puzzling Evidence from the G-7 countries',
Stern School of Business, New York University, Working Paper 17 (1995).

[48] Hachimoto, Y. and Ito, T., 'Effects of Japanese Macroeconomic statistic announcements on the
dollar/yen exchange rate: High-resolution picture', Journal of the Japanese and the International
Economies, 24 (2010), pp. 334-354.
[49] Hetzel, R., 'From the Deutsche Mark to the Euro', Federal Reserve Bank of Richmond, 88 (2002), pp.
29-64.
[50] Hetzel, R., The Monetary Policy of the Federal Reserve: A History (Cambridge, 2008).
[51] Hillebrand, E. and Schnabl, G., 'A Structural Break in the Effects of Japanese Foreign Exchange
Intervention on Yen/Dollar Exchange Rate Volatility', European Central Bank, Working Paper 650
(2006).
[52] Humpage, O., 'Intervention and the Dollar's Decline', Federal Reserve Bank of Cleveland Economic
Review, 7 (1988), pp. 2-16.
[53] Humpage, O. and Osterberg, W., 'Intervention and the foreign exchange risk premium: An empirical
investigation of daily effects', Federal Reserve Bank of Cleveland, Working Paper 9 (1990).
[54] Humpage, O. and Osterberg, W., 'Why Intervention Rarely Works', Federal Reserve Bank of Cleveland, Economic Commentary February (2000).
[55] Ito, T., 'Interventions and Japanese economic recovery', International Economics and Economic Policy, 2 (2005), pp. 219-239.
[56] Ito, T., 'Is Foreign Exchange Intervention Effective? The Japanese experience in the 1990s', The National Bureau of Economic Research, NBER Working Paper 8914 (2002).

[57] Ito, T., 'Myths and Reality of Foreign Exchange Interventions: an application to Japan', International Journal of Finance & Economics, 12 (2007), pp. 133-154.

[58] Ito, T., 'The Yen and the Japanese Economy' in Bergsten, C. and Williamson, J., eds., Dollar Adjustment: How far? Against what? (Washington D.C., 2004), pp. 171-196.

[59] Ito, T. and Sato, K., 'Exchange Rate Changes and Inflation in Post-Crisis Asian Economies: VAR Analysis of Exchange Rate Pass-Through', The National Bureau of Economic Research, NBER Working Paper 12395 (2006).

[60] Ito, T. and Yabu, T., 'What prompts Japan to intervene in the Forex Market? A new approach to a reaction function', Journal of International Money and Finance, 26 (2007), pp. 193-212.

[61] Jacobson, K, 'U.S. Foreign Exchange Operations', Federal Reserve Bank of Kansas City Review, 16 (1990), pp. 37-50.

[62] Johnson, S., Ostry, J., and Subramanian, A., 'The Prospects for Sustained Growth in Africa: Benchmarking the Constraints', International Monetary Fund, IMF Working Paper 52 (2007).

[63] Kaminsky, G. and Lewis, K., 'Does Foreign Exchange Intervention signal future Monetary Policy?', Journal of Monetary Economics, 37 (2007), pp. 285-312.

[64] Kalyvitis, S. and Ifigeneia, S., 'Some empirical evidence on the effects of U.S. monetary shocks on cross exchange rates', Bank of Greece, Working Paper 65 (2008).

[65] Kim, S., 'Monetary policy, foreign exchange intervention, and the exchange rate in a unifying framework', Journal of International Economy, 60 (2003), pp. 355-386.

[66] Klein, M. and Lewis, K., 'Learning about Intervention Target Zones', Journal of International Economics, 35 (1993), pp. 275-295.

[67] Lewis, K., 'Are foreign exchange intervention and monetary policy related and does it really matter?', Journal of Business, 68 (1995), pp. 185-214.

[68] Loretan, M., 'Indexes of the Foreign Exchange Value of the Dollar', Federal Reserve Bulletin, Winter (2005), pp. 1-8.

[69] Lyons, R., The Microstructure Approach to Exchange Rates (Cambridge, MA., 2006).

[70] Meese, R. and Rogoff, K., 'Empirical Exchange Rate Models of the Seventies: Do they fit out of

sample?', Journal of International Economics, 14 (1983), pp. 3-24.

[71] Mussa, M., 'The Role of Official Intervention', Group of Thirty, Occasional Paper 6 (1983).

[72] Neely, C., 'A Foreign Exchange Intervention in an Era of Restraint', Federal Reserve Bank of St. Louis

Review, 93 (2011), pp. 303-324.

[73] Neely, C., 'An Analysis of Recent Studies of the Effect of Foreign Exchange Interventions', Federal

Reserve Bank of St. Louis Review, 87 (2005), pp. 685-717.

[74] Neely, C., 'Central Bank Authorities' Beliefs about Foreign Exchange Intervention', Federal Reserve Bank of St. Louis, Working Paper 45 (2006).

[75] Neely, C., 'The Practice of Central Bank Intervention: Looking Under the Hood', Federal Reserve Bank of St. Louis Review, 83 (2001), pp. 1-10.

[76] Neumann, M., 'Intervention in the Mark/Dollar Market: the Authorities' Reaction Function', Journal of International Money and Finance, 3 (1984), pp. 223-239.

[77] Neumann, M. and Hagen, J., 'Monetary Policy in Germany', Indiana Centre for Global Business, Indiana University, Discussion Paper 59 (1991).

[78] Obstfeld, M., 'The Effectiveness of Foreign-Exchange Intervention: Recent Experience, 1985-1988', in Branson, W., Frenkel, J., and Goldstein, M., eds., International Policy Coordination and Exchange Rate Fluctuations (Chicago, IL., 1990), pp. 197-246.

[79] Obstfeld, M., 'The Yen and Japan's Economy, 1985-2007', Columbia Business School Centre on Japanese Economy and Business, Working Paper 269 (2009).

[80] Orphanides, A., 'Monetary-Policy Rules and the Great Inflation', American Economic Review, 92 (2002), pp. 115-120.

[81] Ozcelebi, O. and Yildirim, N., 'Revisiting the relationship between exchange rates and output with SVAR Blanchard-Quah framework: empirical evidence from Turkey, Germany and Russia', Economic and Business Review, 13 (2011), pp. 179-198.

[82] Popper, H. and Montgomery, J., 'Information Sharing and Central Bank Intervention in Foreign- Exchange Market', Journal of International Economics, 55 (2001), pp. 295-316.

[83] Ramaswamy, R. and Samiei, H., 'The Yen-Dollar Rate: Have Interventions Mattered?', International Monetary Fund, IMF Working Paper 00 (1995).

[84] Rodrik, D., 'The Real Exchange Rate and Economic Growth', Weatherhead Center for International Affairs, Harvard University, WCFIA Working Paper 141 (2008).

[85] Rogoff, K., 'The failure of empirical exchange rate models: no longer new, but still true', Economic Policy Web Essay

[86] Romer, C. and Romer, D., 'The evolution of economic understanding and Postwar stabilization policy', The National Bureau of Economic Research, NBER Working Paper 9274 (2002).

[87] Sarno, L. and Taylor, M., The Economics of Exchange Rates (Cambridge, 2002).

[88] Sarno, L. and Taylor, M., 'Official Intervention in the Foreign Exchange Market: Is It Effective and, If So, How Does It Work?', Journal of Economic Literature, 39 (2001), pp. 839–868.

[89] Schwartz, A., 'US Foreign Exchange Market Intervention since 1962', Scottish Journal of Political
Economy, 43 (1996), pp. 379-397.

[90] Shleifer, A. and Vishny, R., 'The limits of Arbitrage', The National Bureau of Economic Research,
NBER Working Paper 5167 (1995).

[91] Silber, Volcker: The Triumph of Persistence (New York, 2012).

[92] Vitale, P., 'Sterilized Central Bank Intervention in the Foreign Exchange Market', Journal of International Economics, 49 (1999), pp. 245-267.

[Page intentionally left blank]

[Page intentionally left blank]

www.ingramcontent.com/pod-product-compliance
Lightning Source LLC
Chambersburg PA
CBHW020656220526
45464CB00001B/455